D0830853

First published in the UK in 2019 by Studio Press Books,
an imprint of of Bonnier Books UK,
The Plaza, 535 King's Road, London, SW10 0SZ

www.studiopressbooks.co.uk
www.bonnierbooks.co.uk

All images © Tim Whyatt 2019

3 5 7 9 10 8 6 4 2

ISBN 978-1-78741-579-9

Printed in Italy

SENIOR MOMENTS

Older But No Wiser

STUDIO PRESS

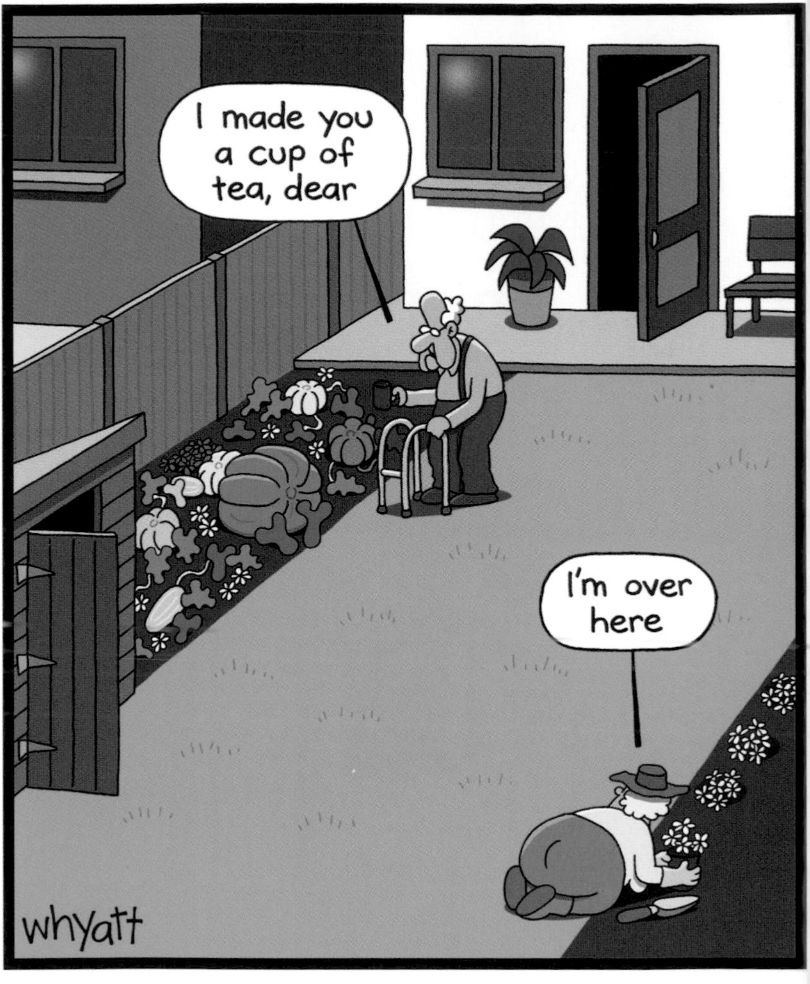
I made you a cup of tea, dear
I'm over here
whyatt

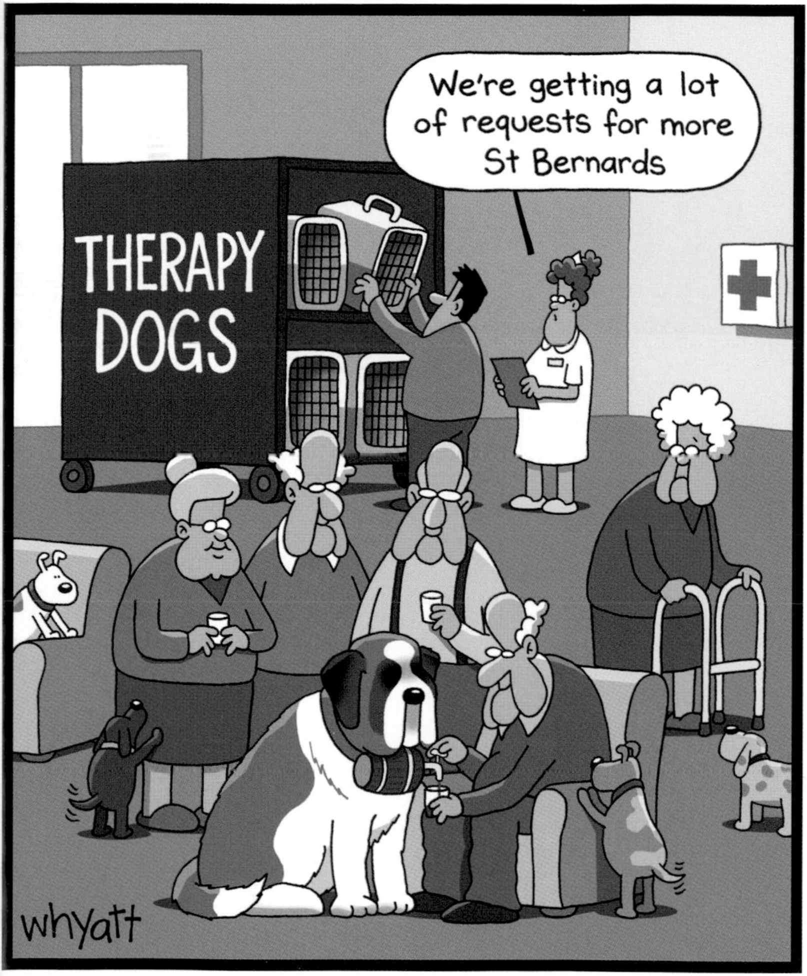
We're getting a lot of requests for more St Bernards
THERAPY DOGS
whyatt

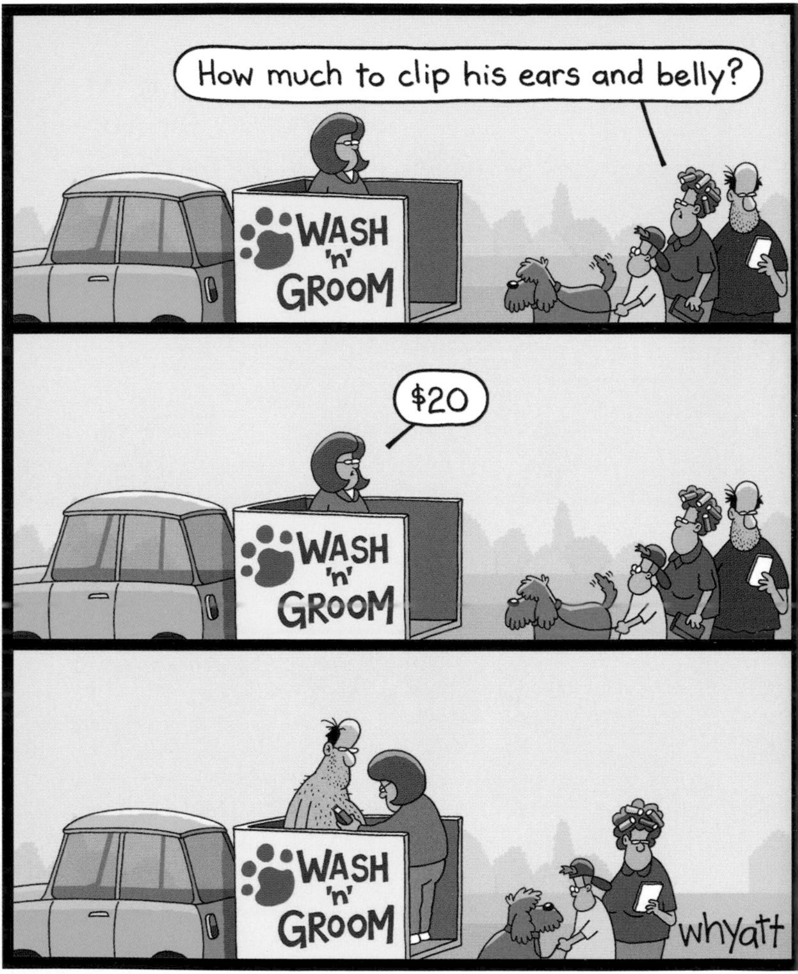
How much to clip his ears and belly?
WASH 'n' GROOM
$20
WASH 'n' GROOM
WASH 'n' GROOM
whyatt

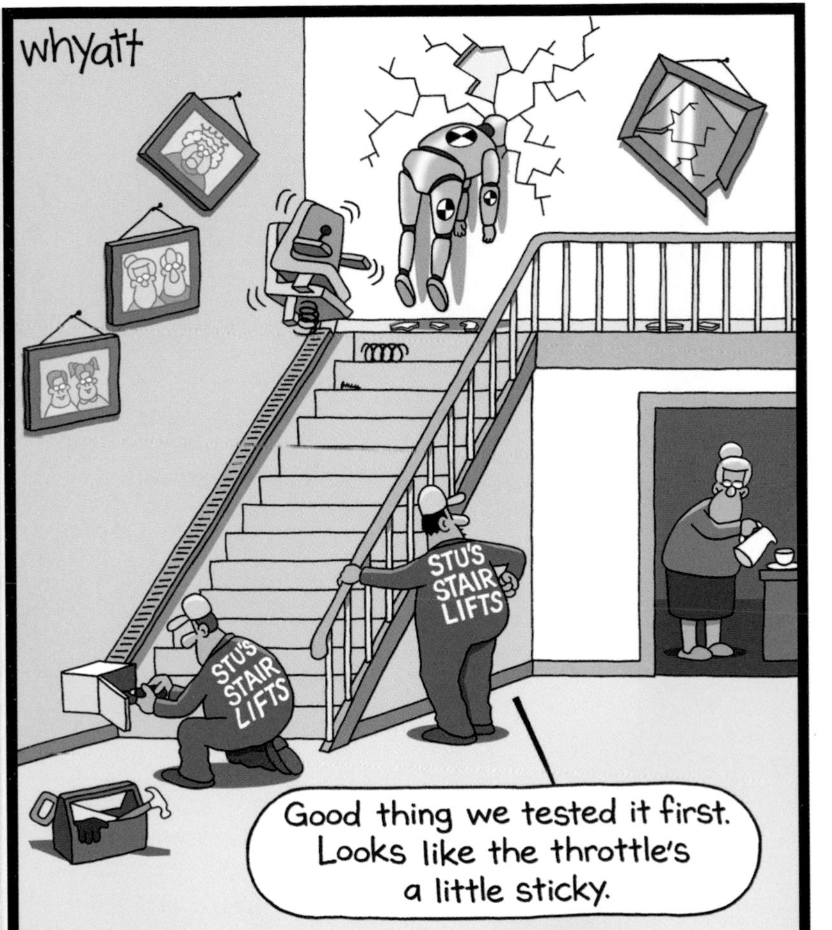
whyatt
STU'S STAIR LIFTS
STU'S STAIR LIFTS
Good thing we tested it first. Looks like the throttle's a little sticky.

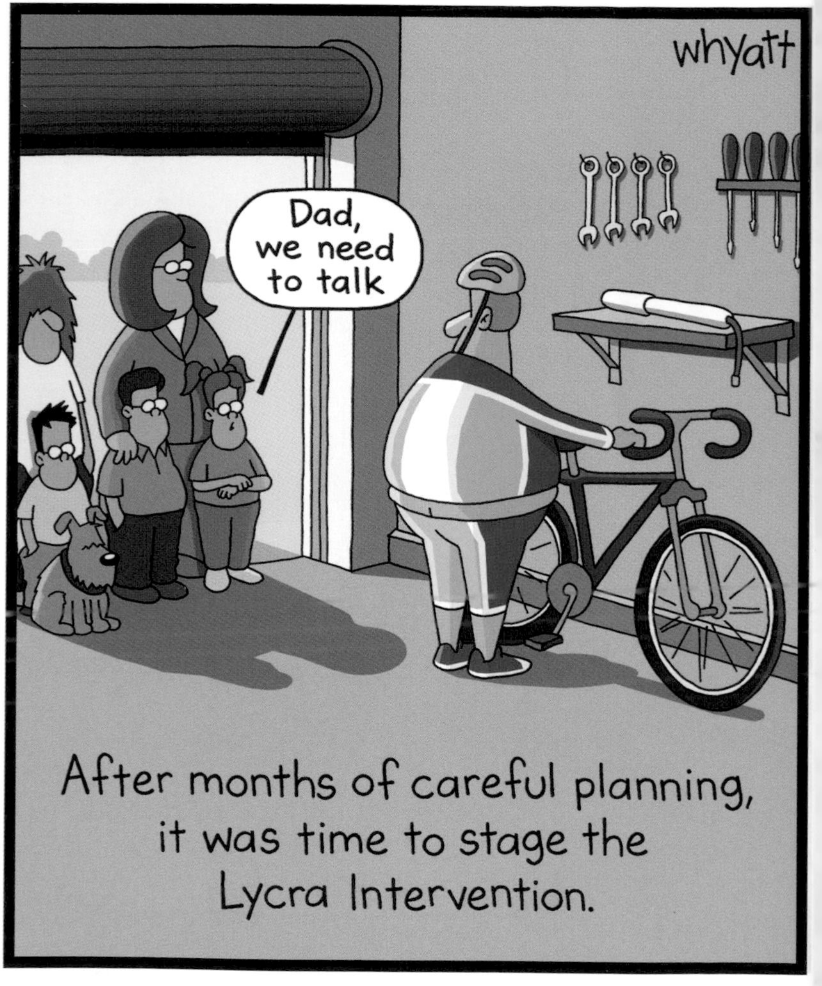
whyatt
Dad, we need to talk

After months of careful planning, it was time to stage the Lycra Intervention.

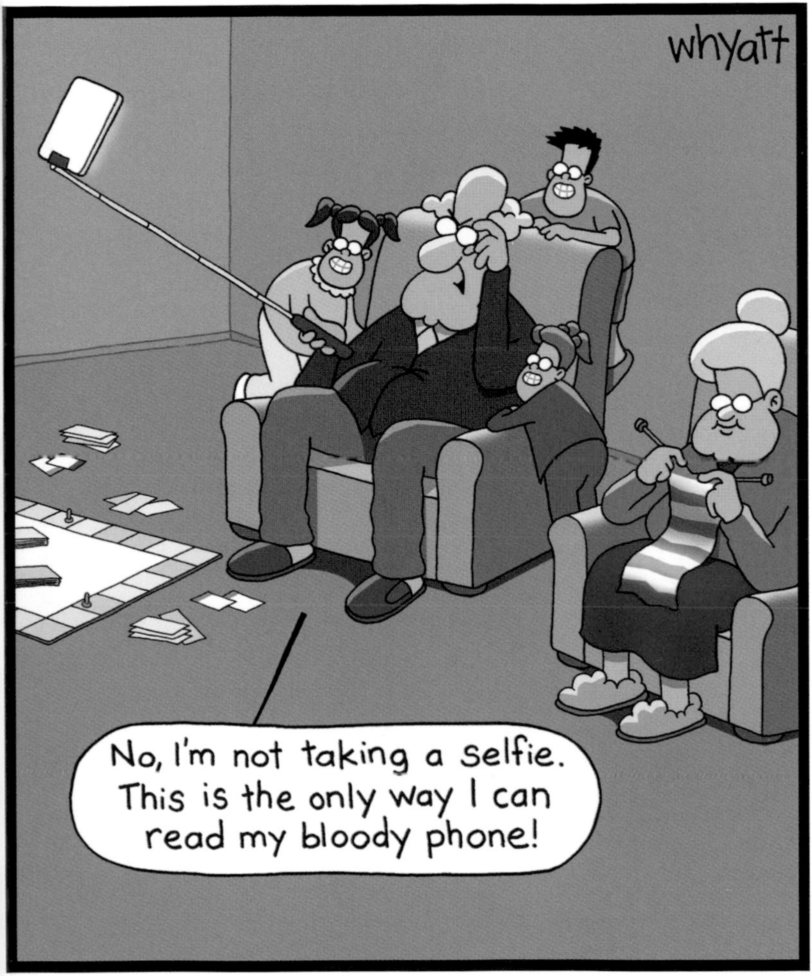
whyatt
No, I'm not taking a selfie.
This is the only way I can
read my bloody phone!

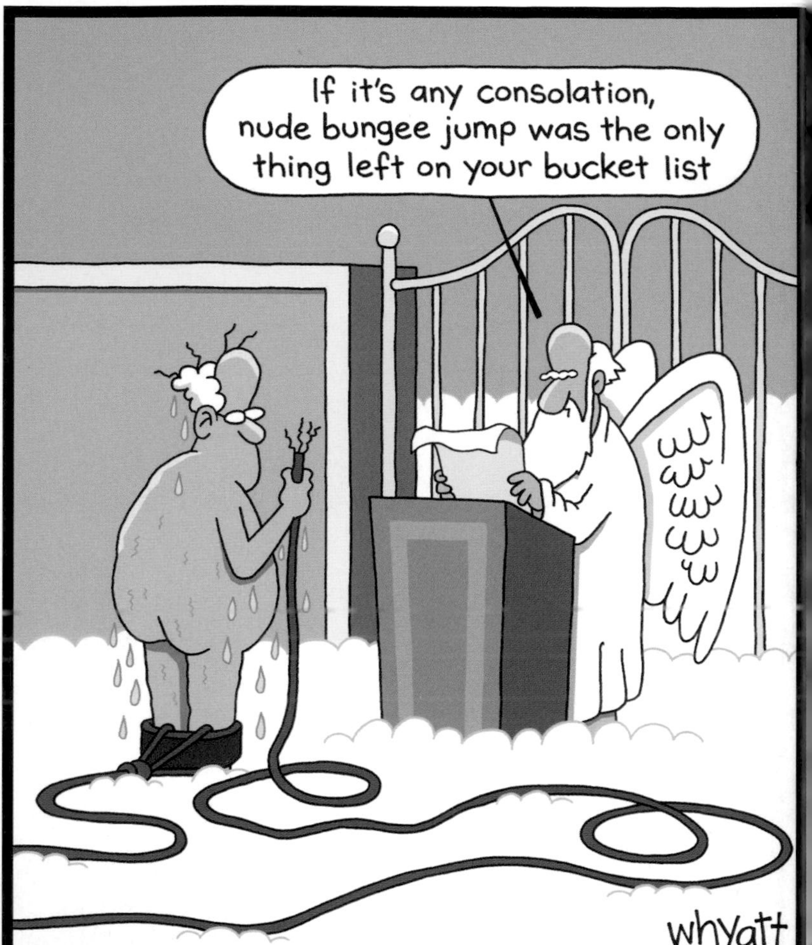
If it's any consolation, nude bungee jump was the only thing left on your bucket list
whyatt

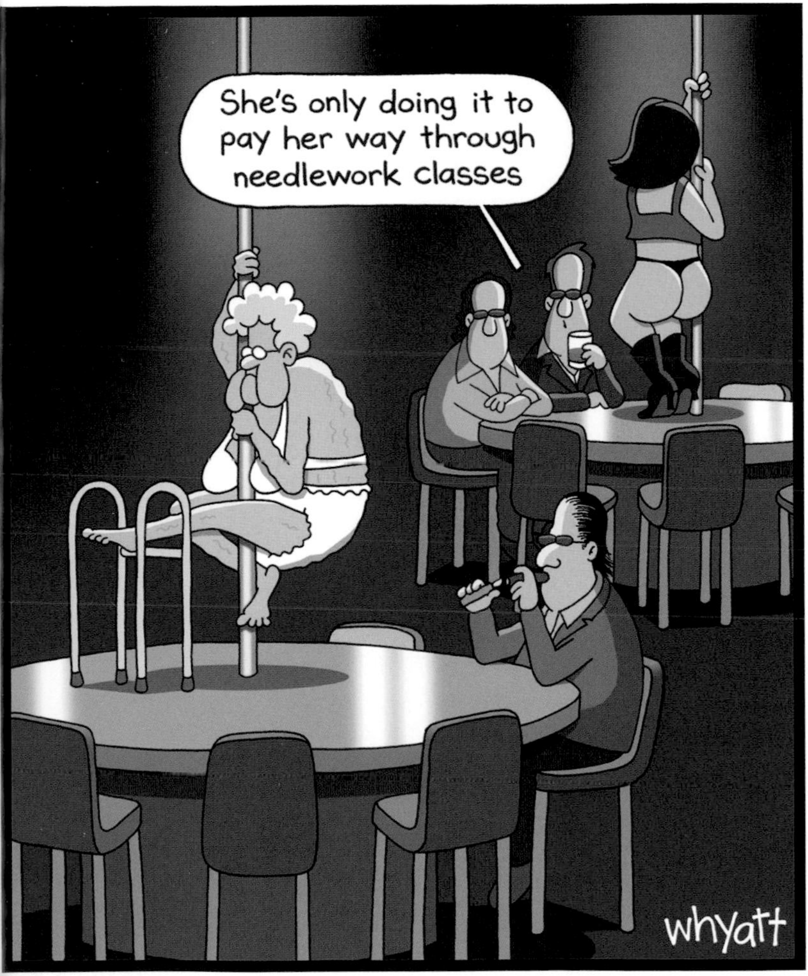
She's only doing it to pay her way through needlework classes
whyatt

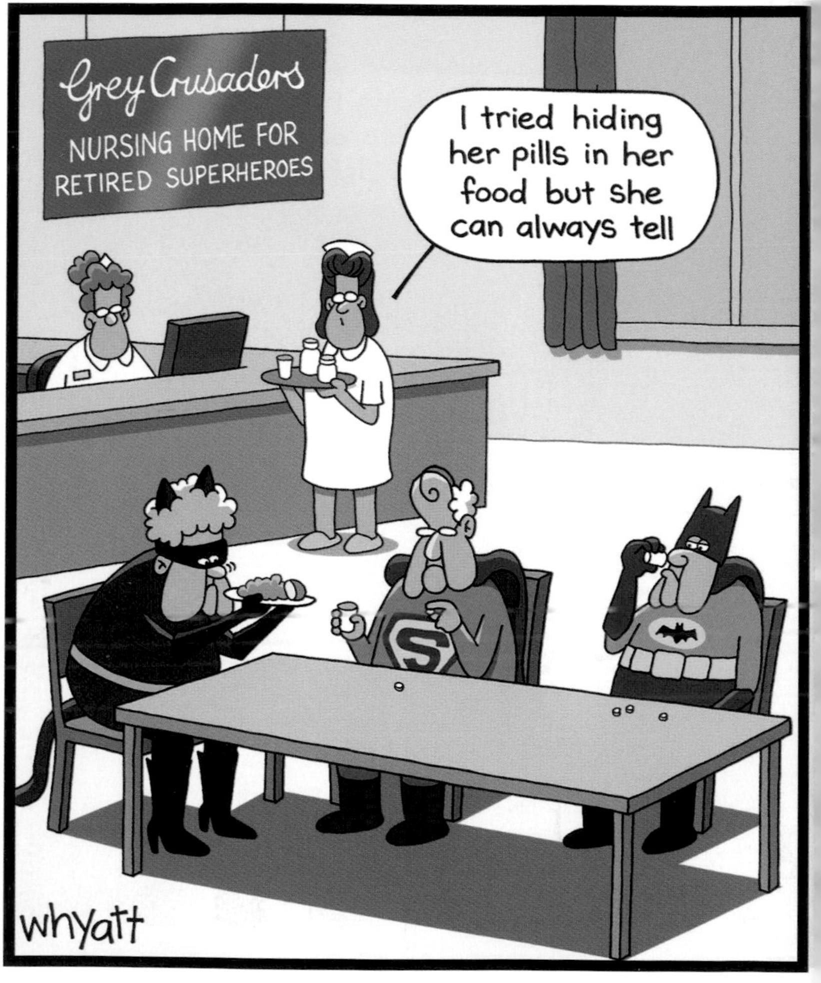
Grey Crusaders
NURSING HOME FOR
RETIRED SUPERHEROES
I tried hiding her pills in her food but she can always tell
S
whyatt

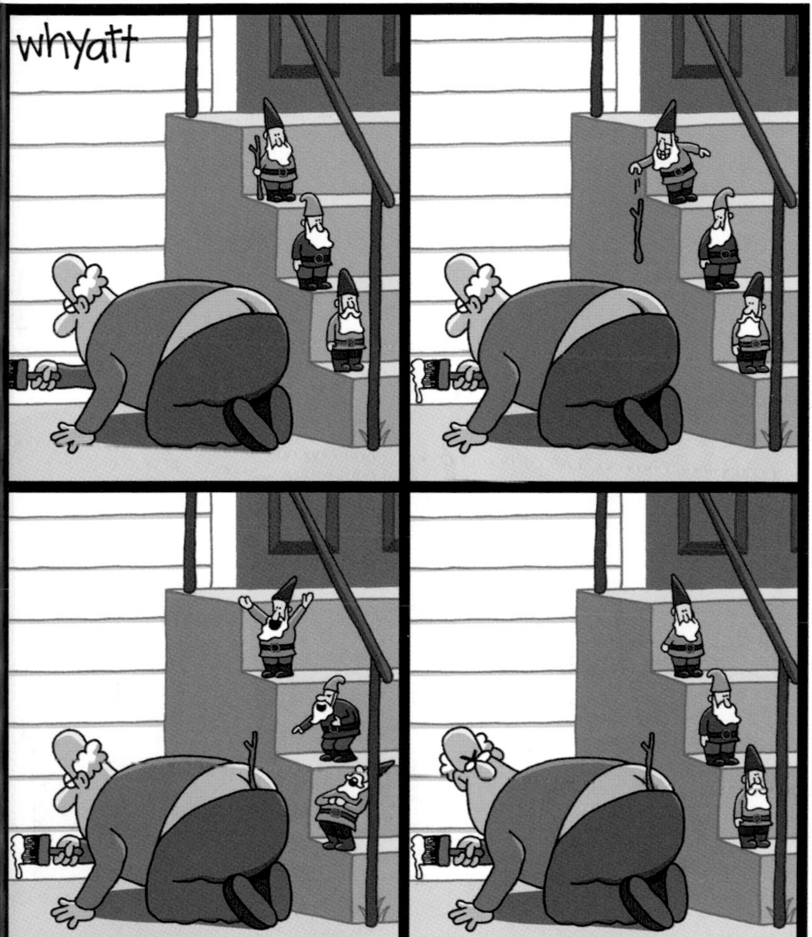
whyatt

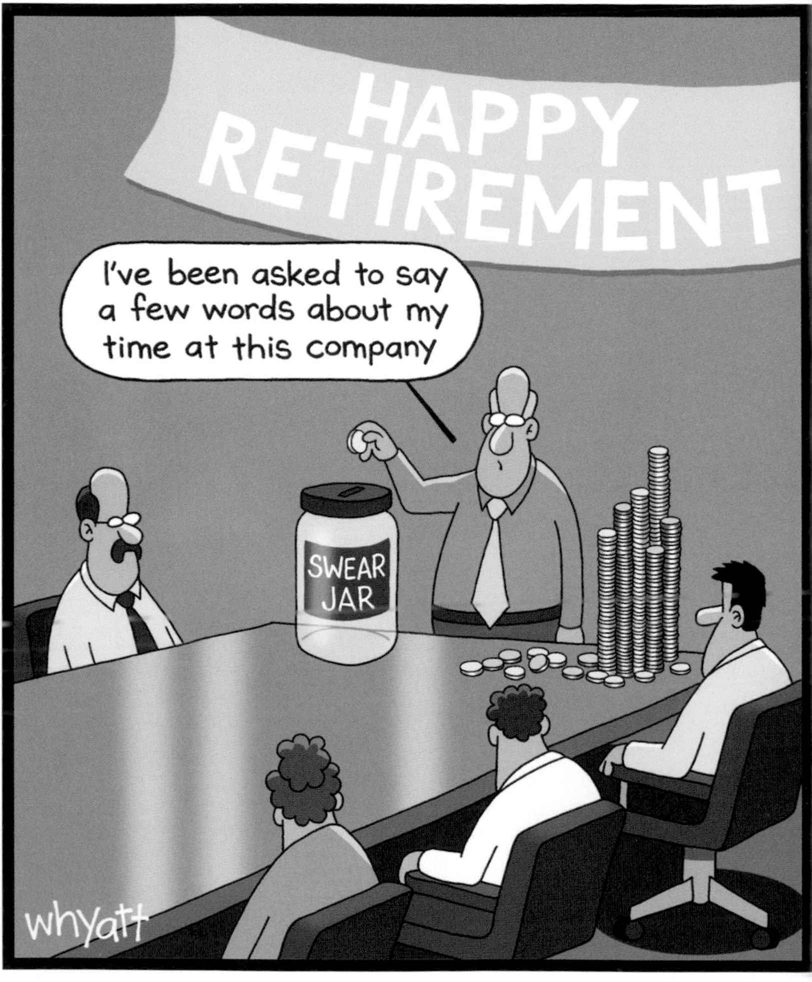
HAPPY RETIREMENT
I've been asked to say a few words about my time at this company
SWEAR JAR
whyatt

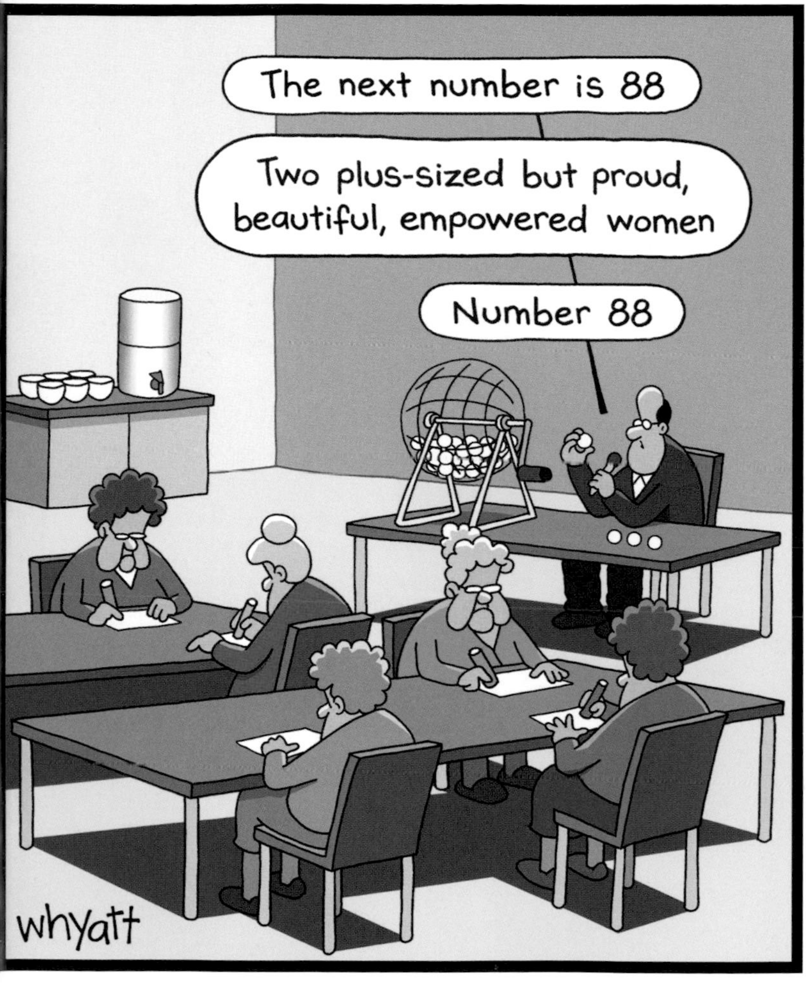
The next number is 88
Two plus-sized but proud, beautiful, empowered women
Number 88
whyatt

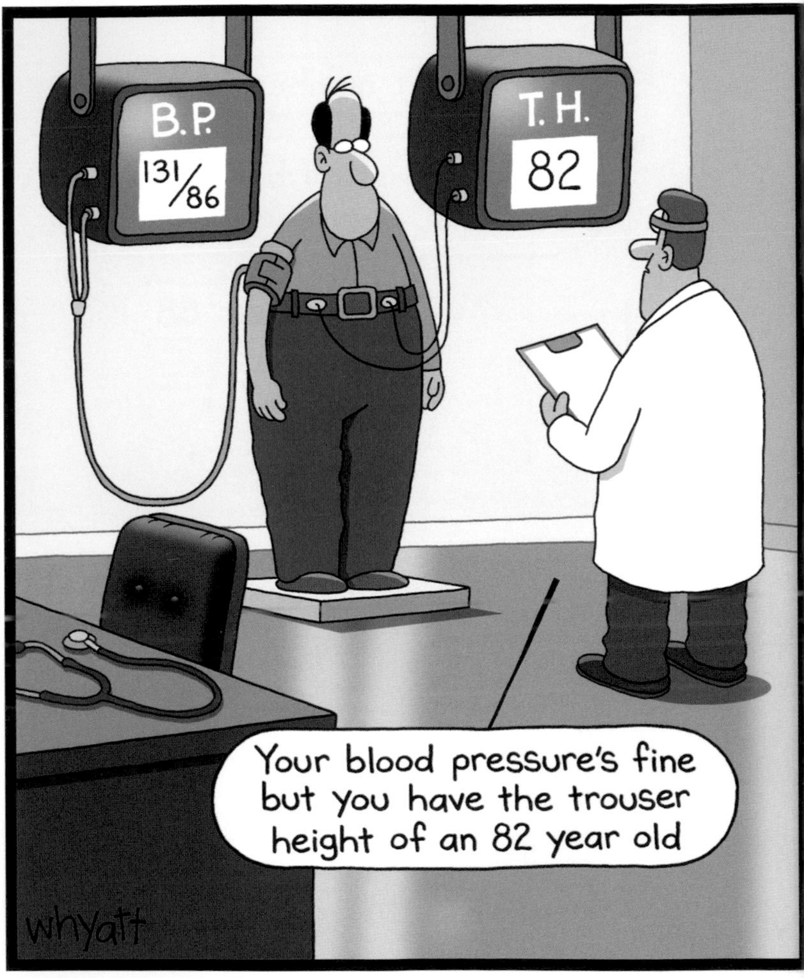
B.P.
131/86
T.H.
82
Your blood pressure's fine but you have the trouser height of an 82 year old
whyatt

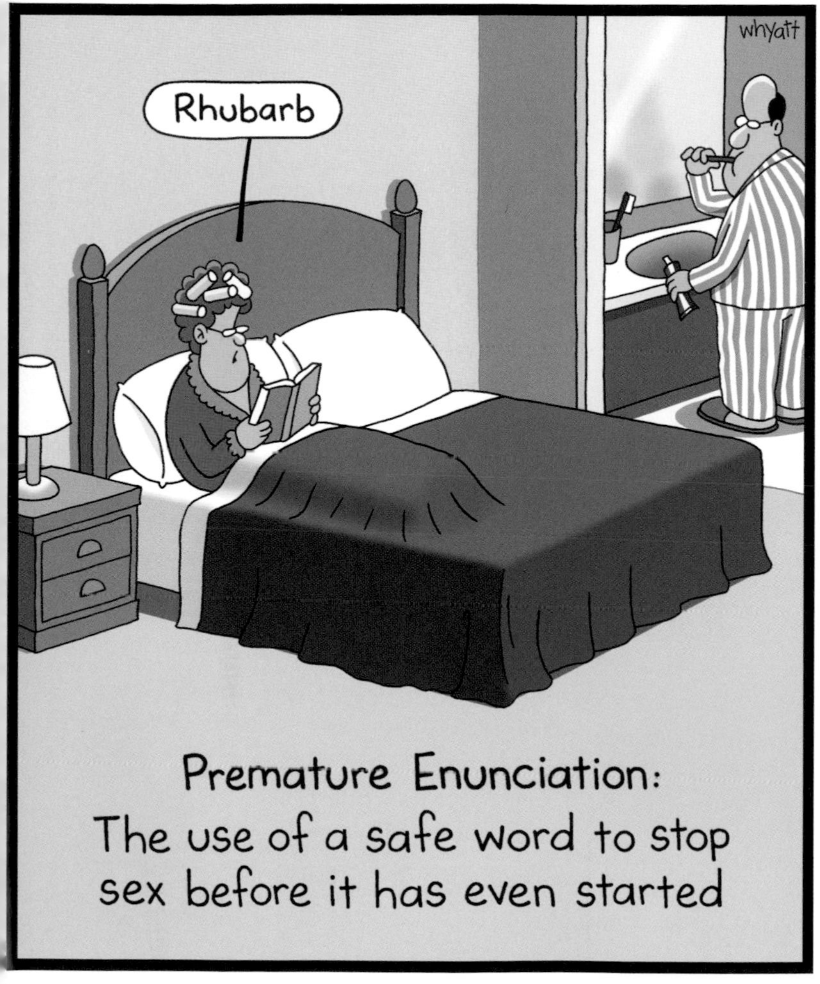
whyatt
Rhubarb

Premature Enunciation:
The use of a safe word to stop sex before it has even started

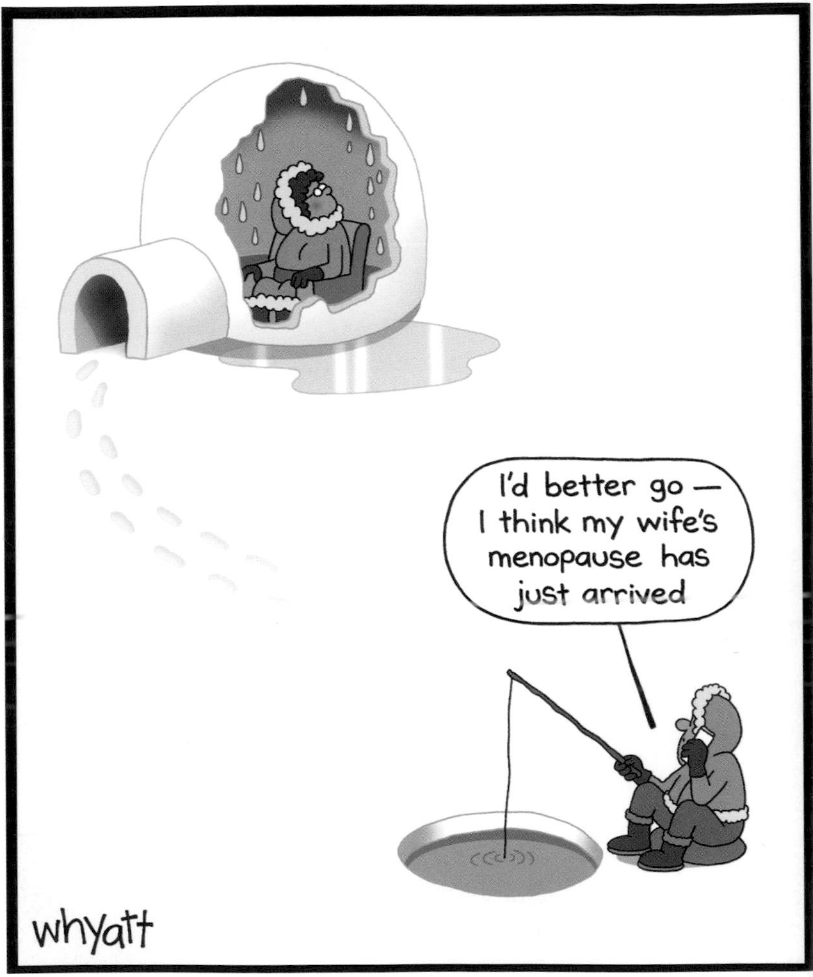
I'd better go — I think my wife's menopause has just arrived
whyatt

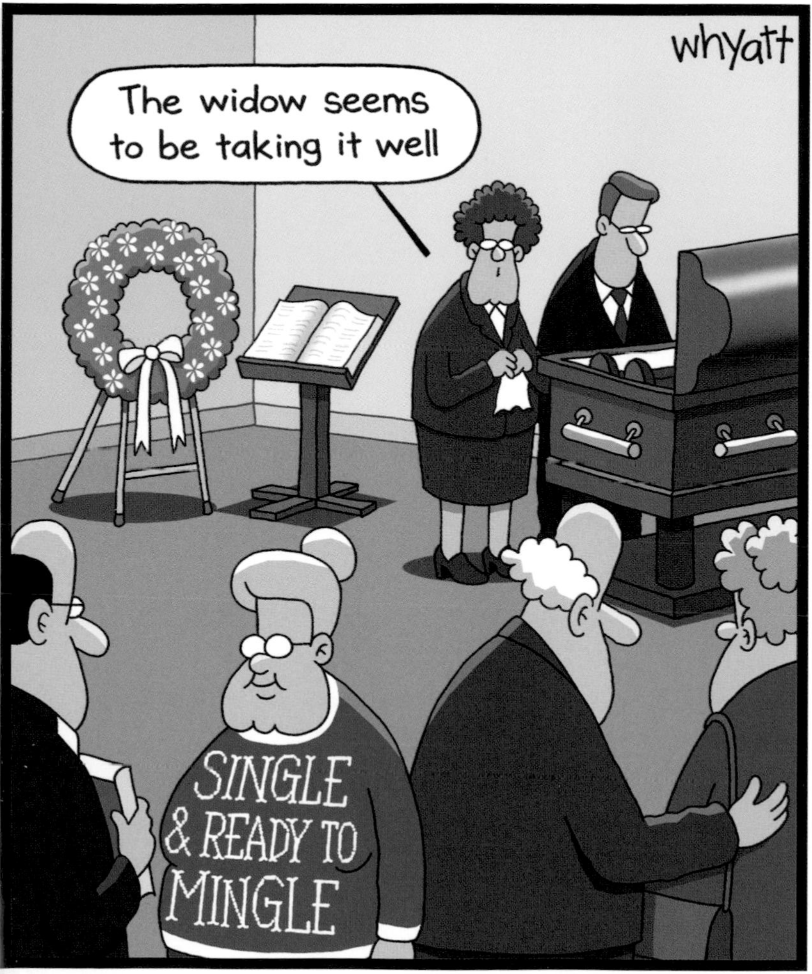
whyatt
The widow seems to be taking it well
SINGLE & READY TO MINGLE

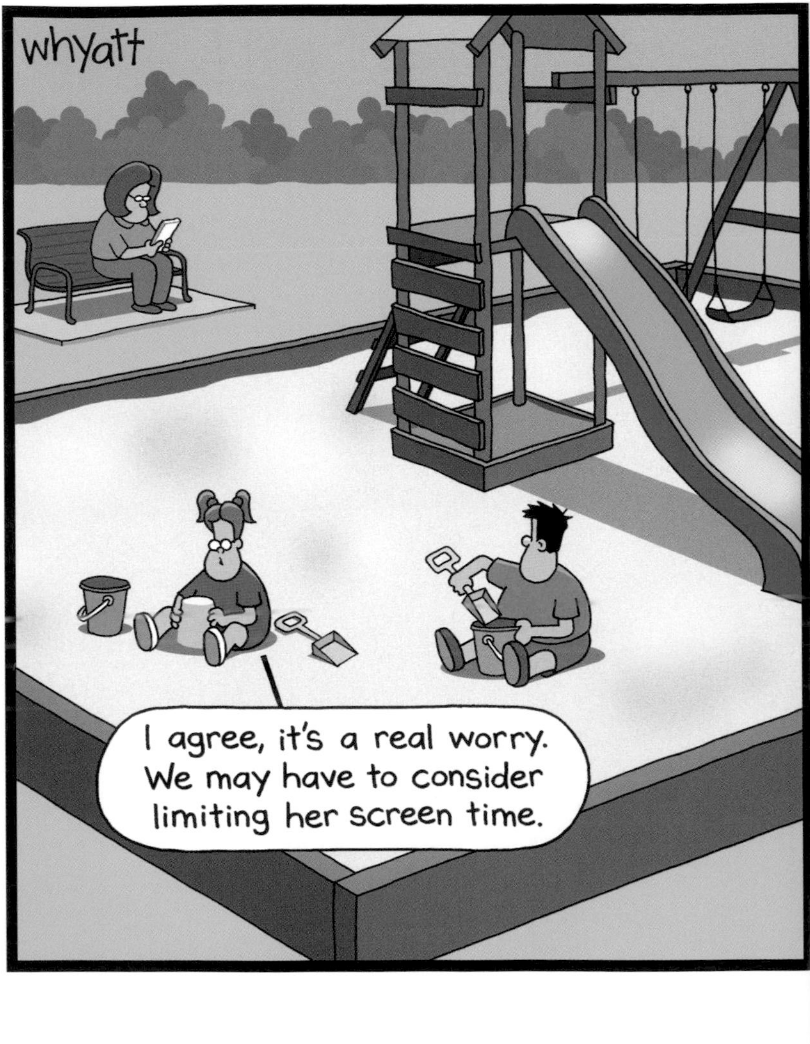
whyatt
I agree, it's a real worry. We may have to consider limiting her screen time.

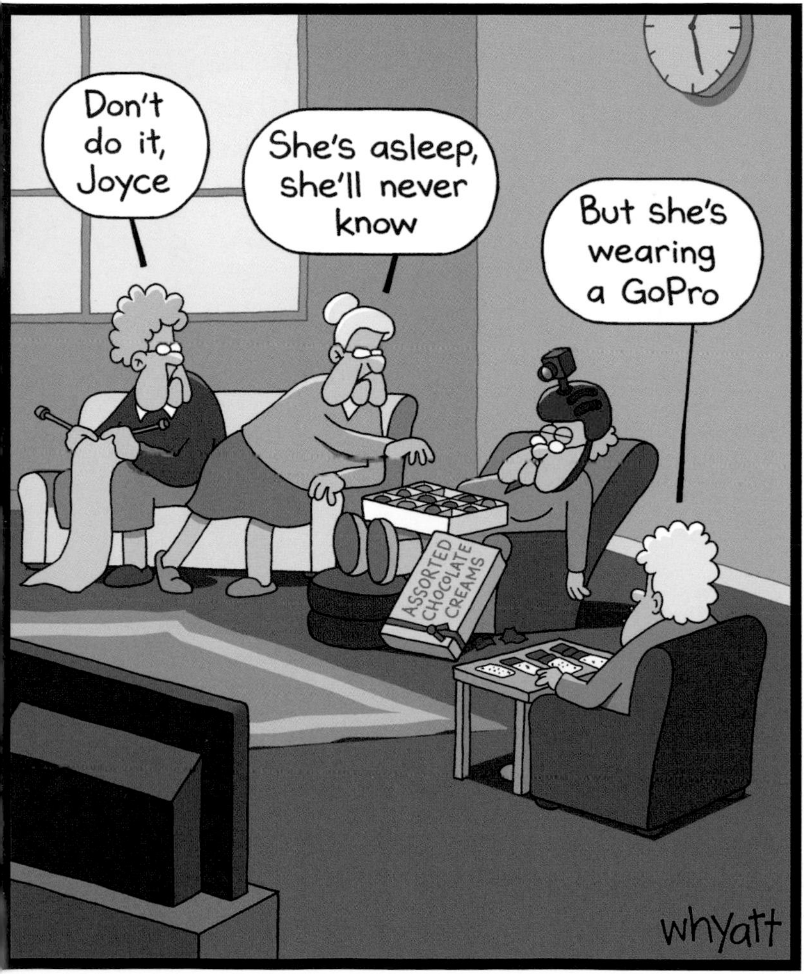
Don't do it, Joyce
She's asleep, she'll never know
But she's wearing a GoPro
ASSORTED CHOCOLATE CREAMS
whyatt

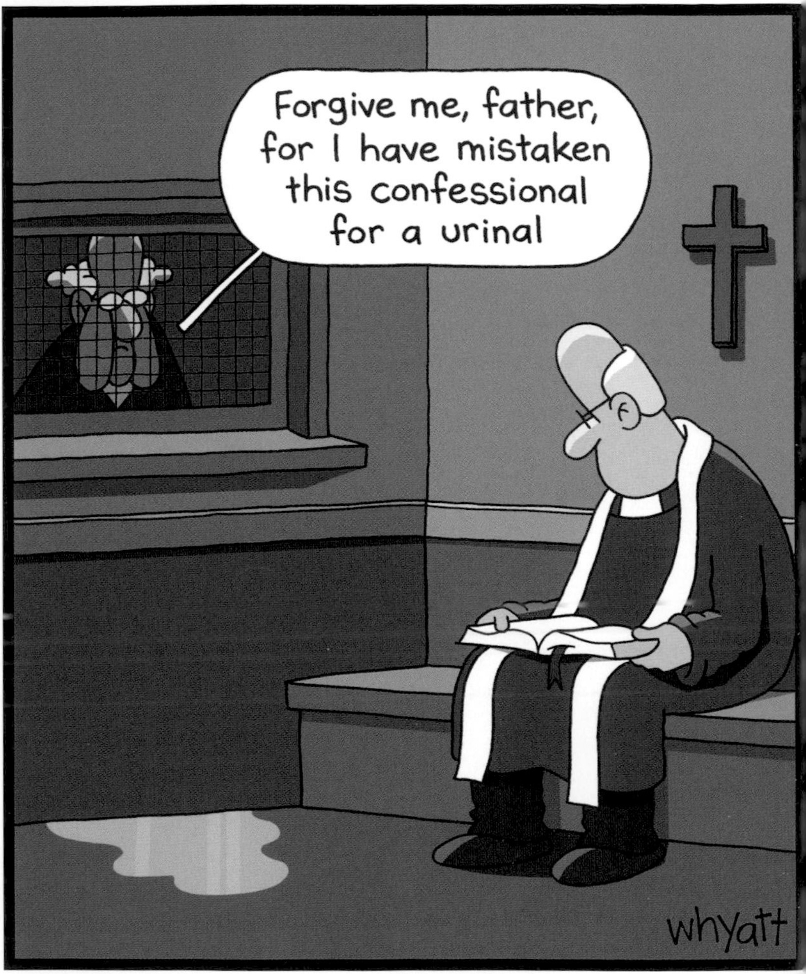
Forgive me, father, for I have mistaken this confessional for a urinal
whyatt

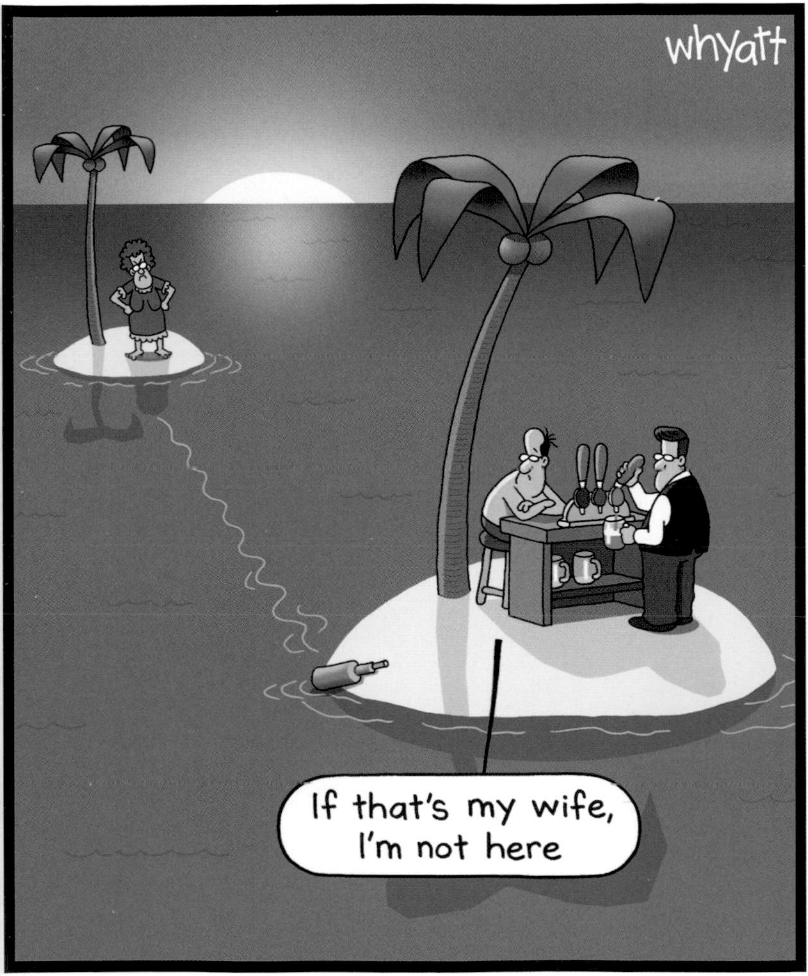
whyatt
If that's my wife, I'm not here

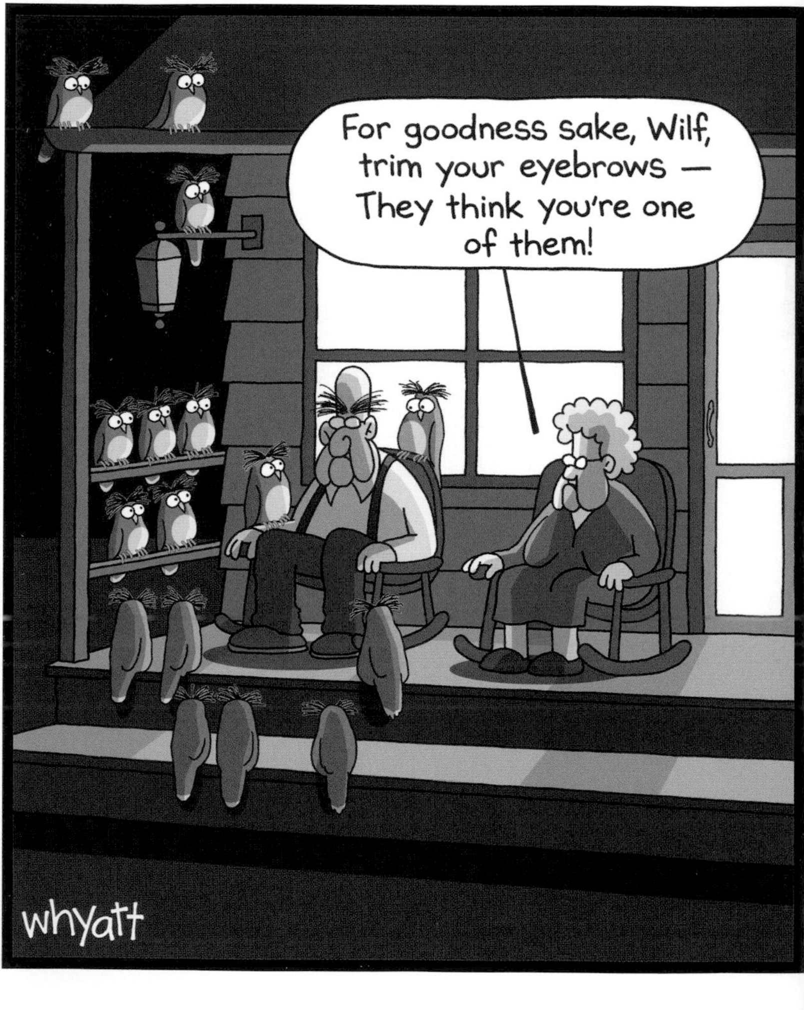
For goodness sake, Wilf, trim your eyebrows — They think you're one of them!
whyatt

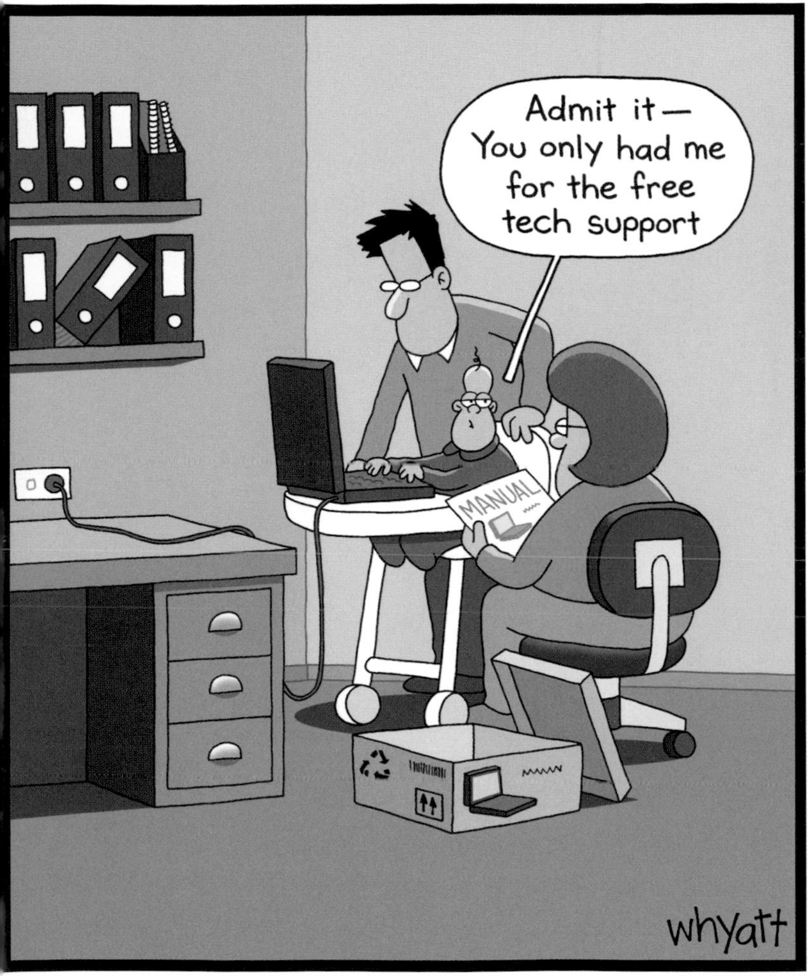
Admit it— You only had me for the free tech support
MANUAL
whyatt

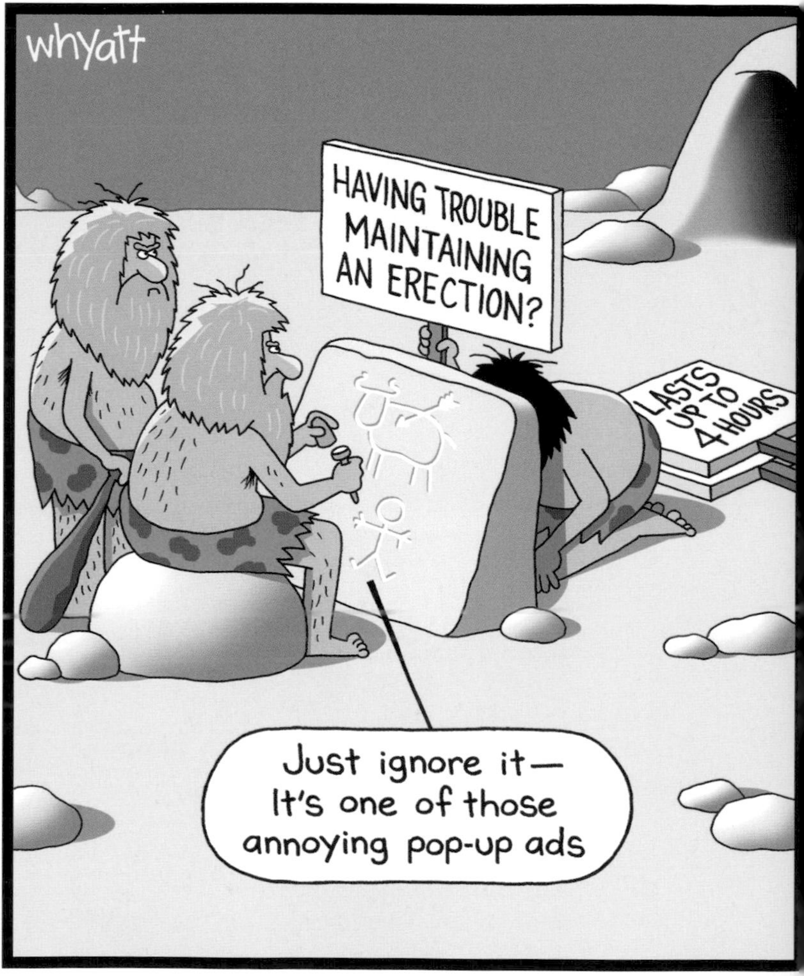
whyatt
HAVING TROUBLE MAINTAINING AN ERECTION?
LASTS UP TO 4 HOURS
Just ignore it—
It's one of those
annoying pop-up ads

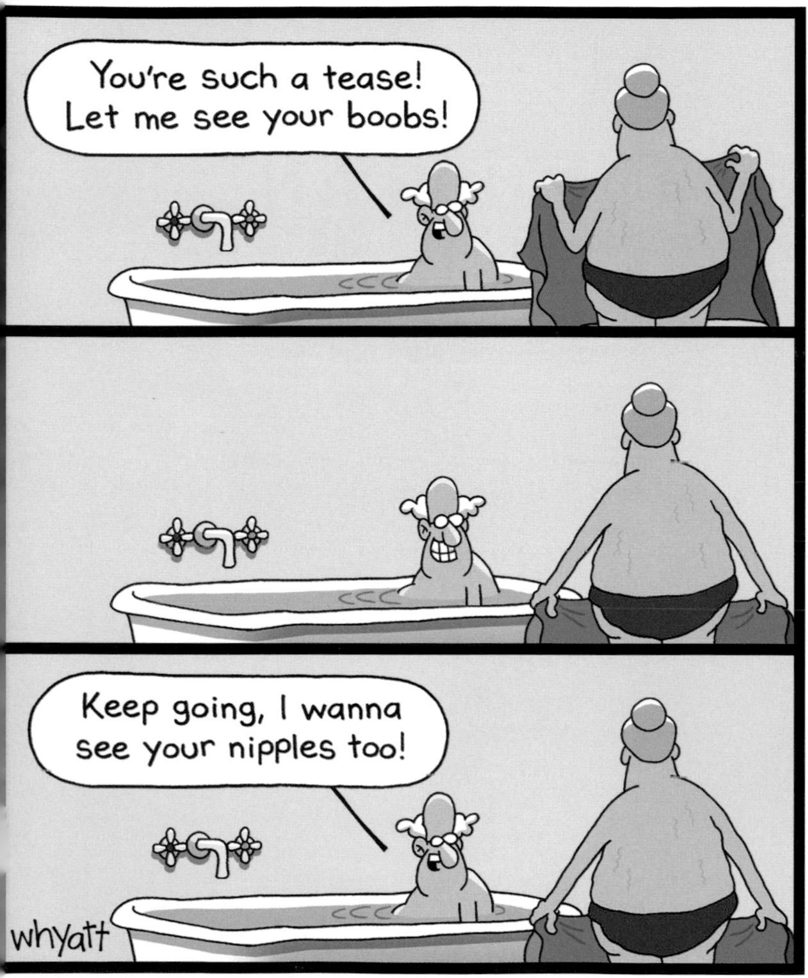
You're such a tease! Let me see your boobs!
Keep going, I wanna see your nipples too!
whyatt

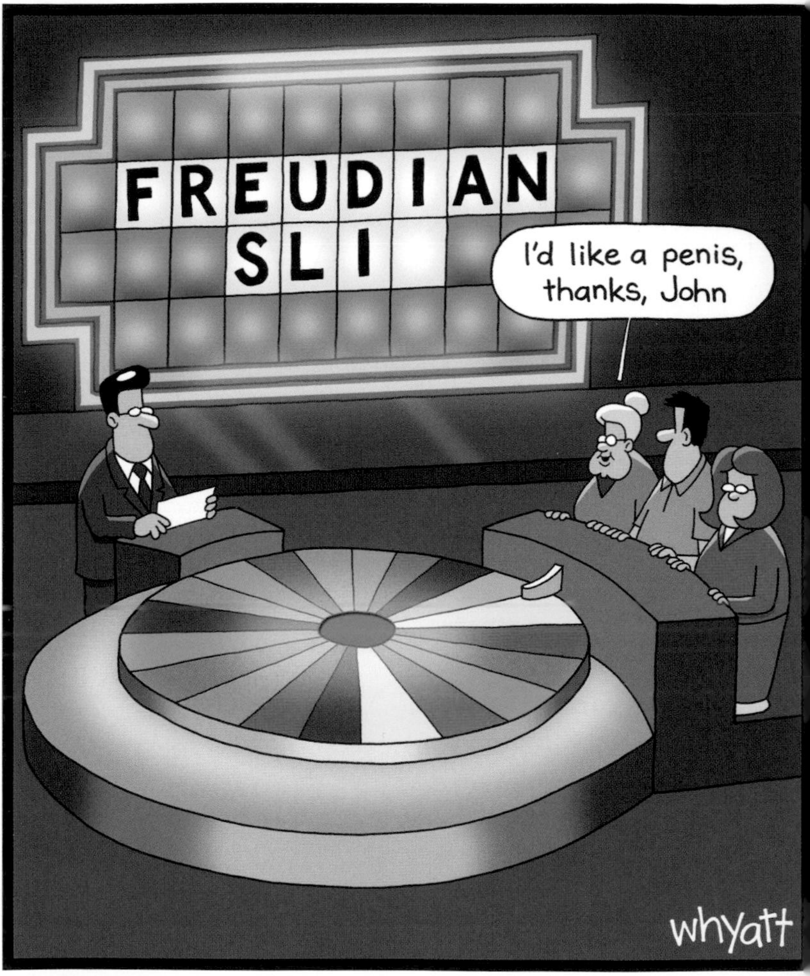
FREUDIAN
SLI
I'd like a penis, thanks, John
whyatt

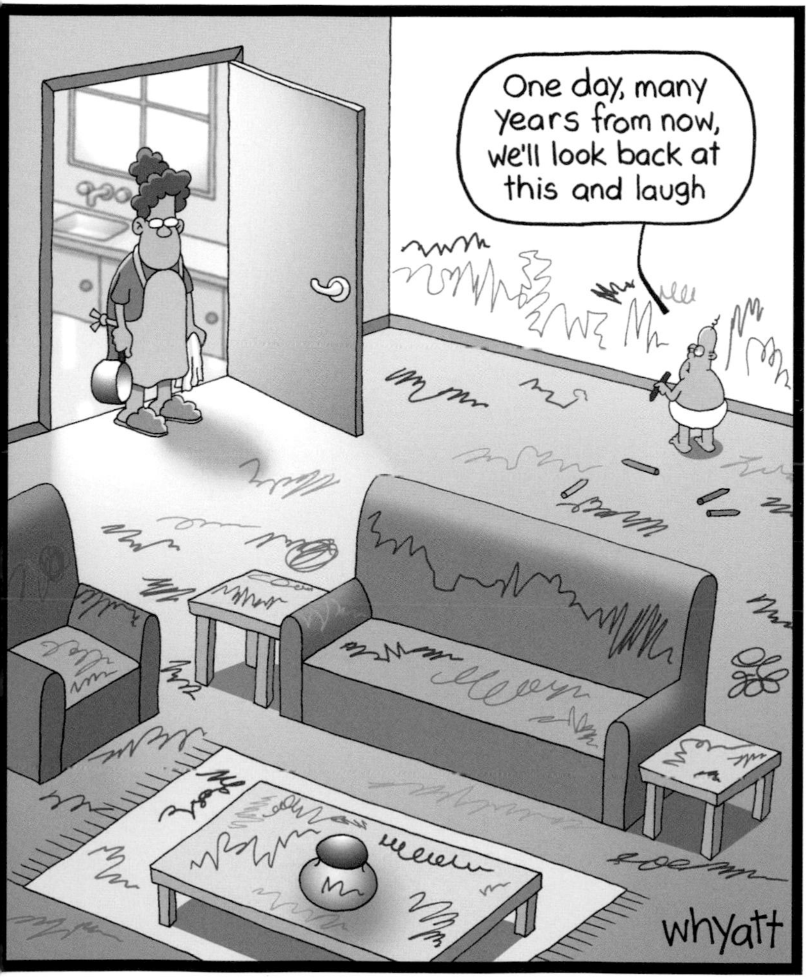
One day, many years from now, we'll look back at this and laugh
whyatt

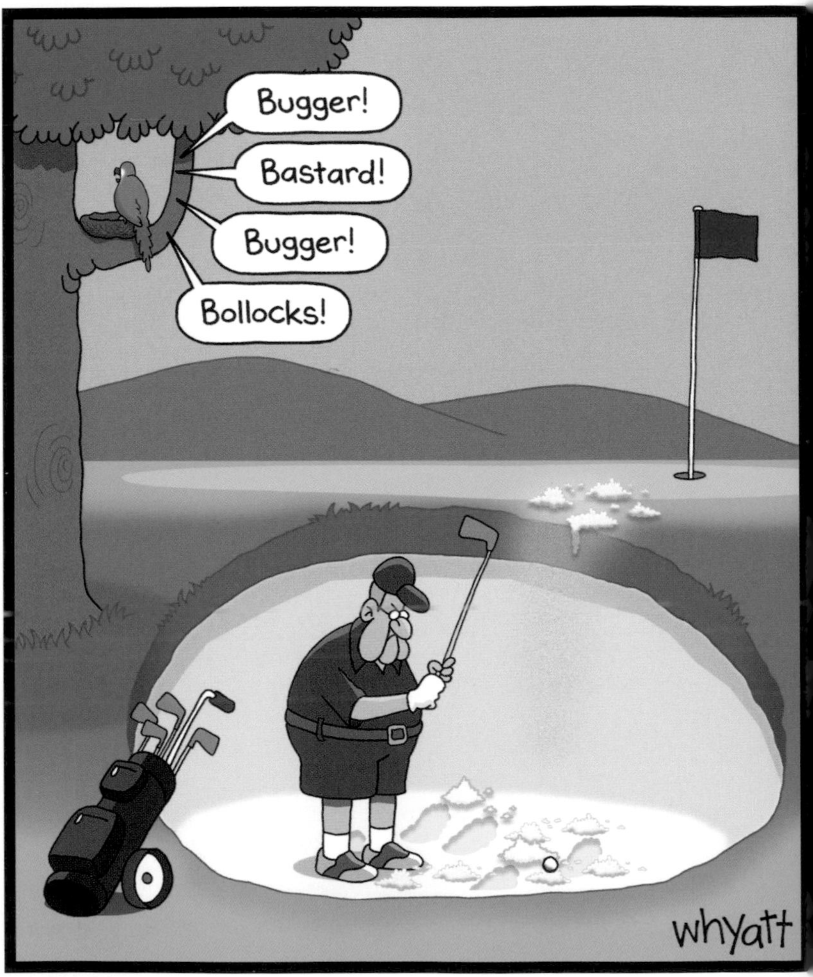
Bugger!
Bastard!
Bugger!
Bollocks!
whyatt

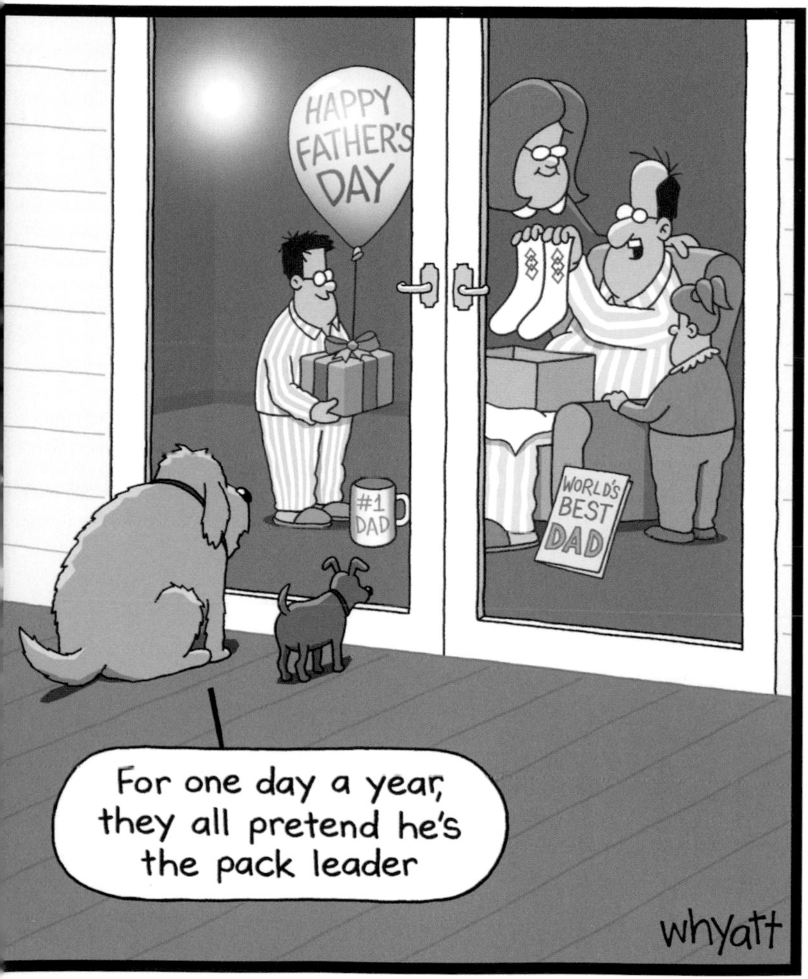
HAPPY FATHER'S DAY
#1 DAD
WORLD'S BEST DAD
For one day a year, they all pretend he's the pack leader
whyatt

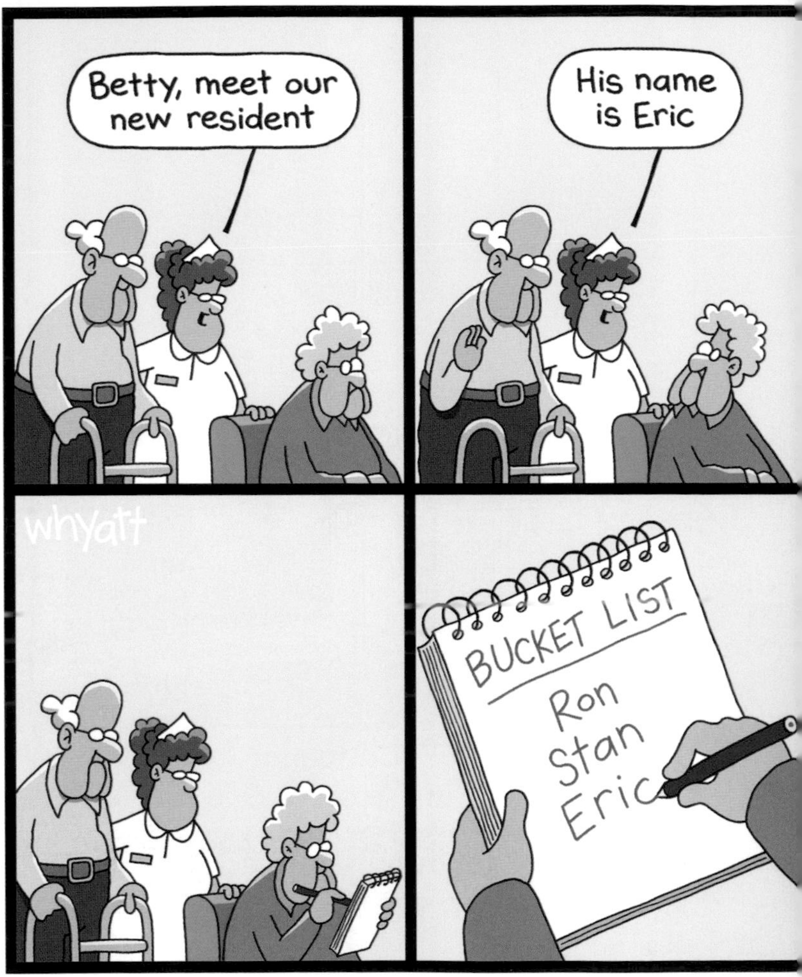
Betty, meet our new resident
His name is Eric
whyatt
BUCKET LIST
Ron
Stan
Eric

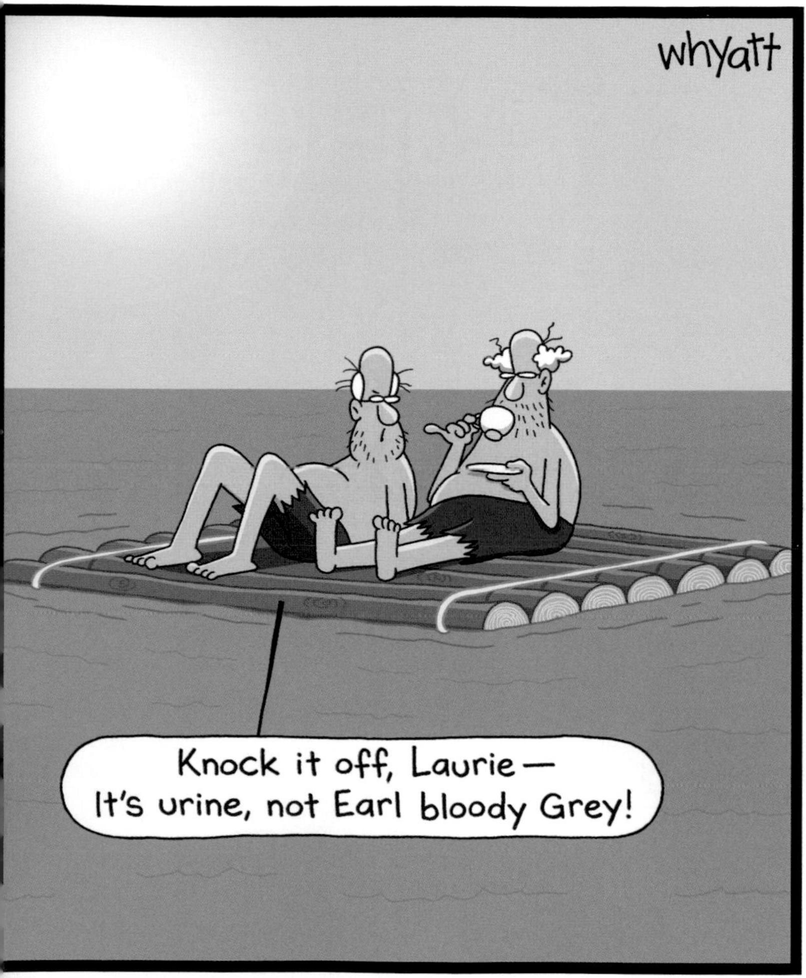
whyatt
Knock it off, Laurie —
It's urine, not Earl bloody Grey!

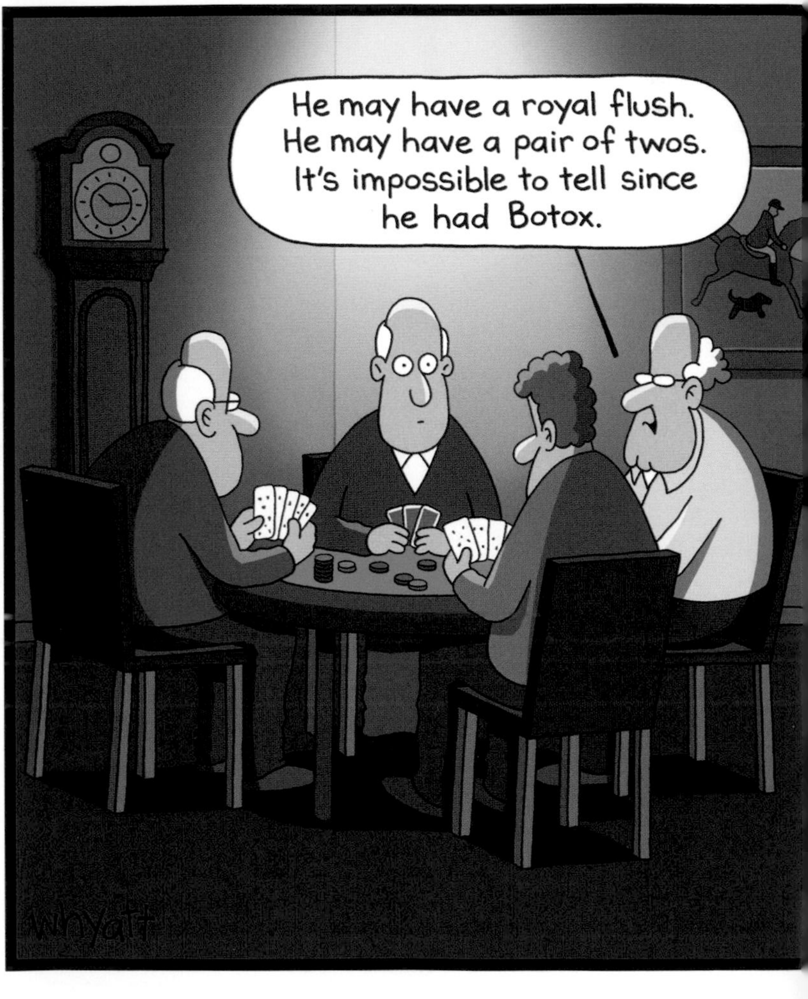
He may have a royal flush. He may have a pair of twos. It's impossible to tell since he had Botox.
Whyatt

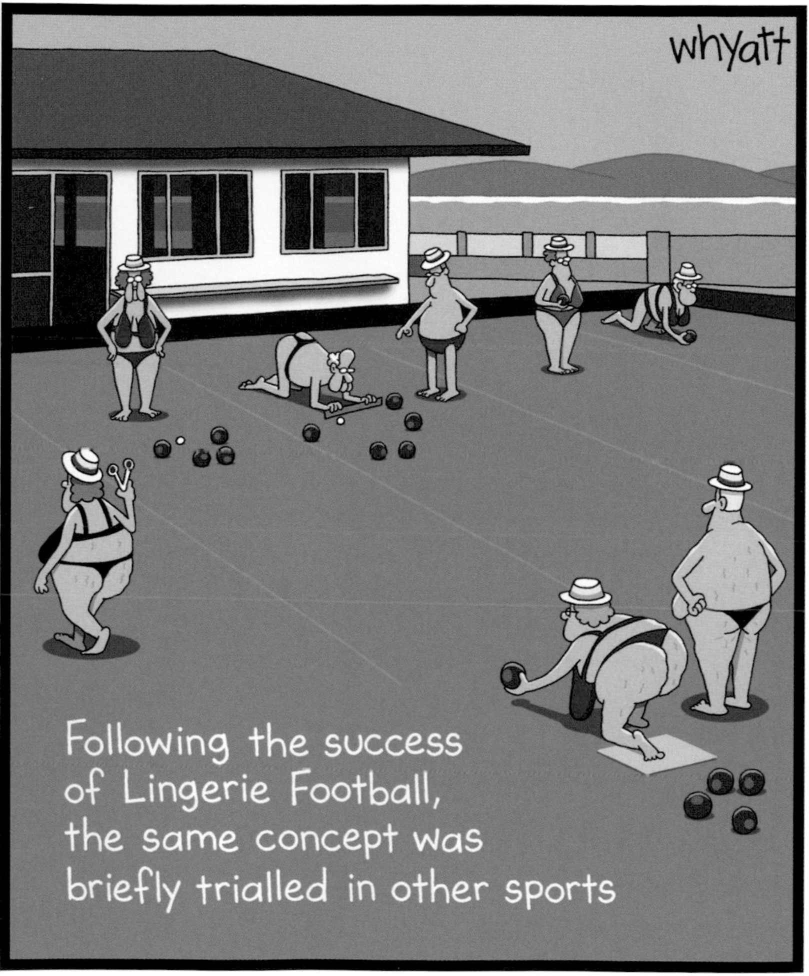
whyatt
Following the success
of Lingerie Football,
the same concept was
briefly trialled in other sports

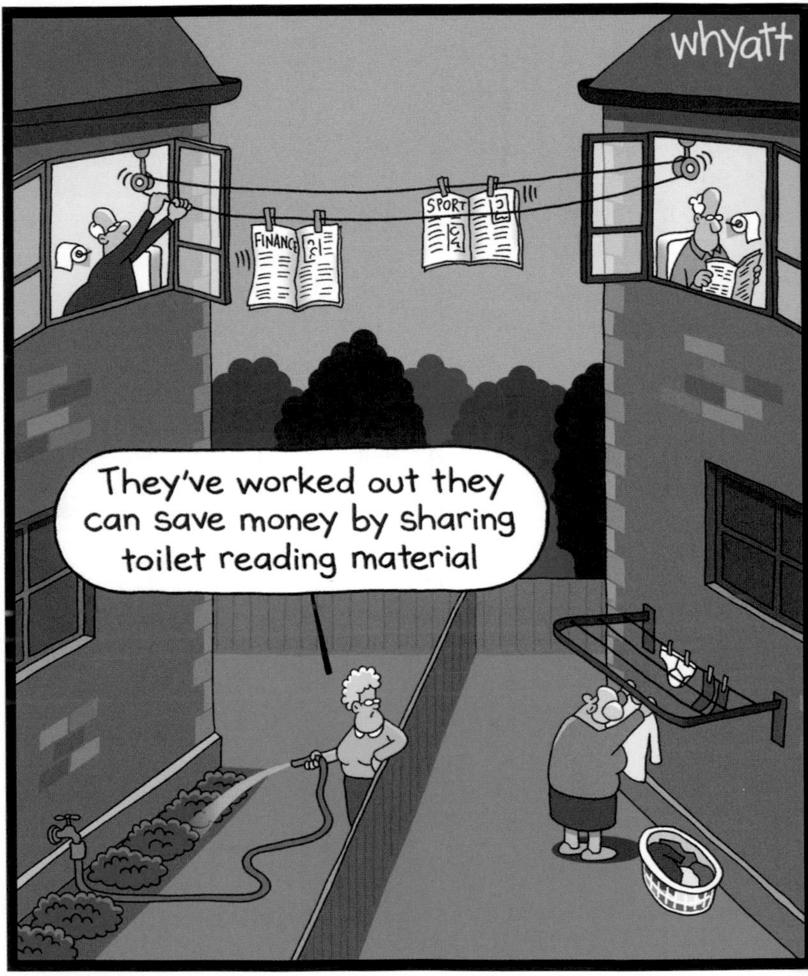
whyatt
SPORT
FINANCE
They've worked out they can save money by sharing toilet reading material

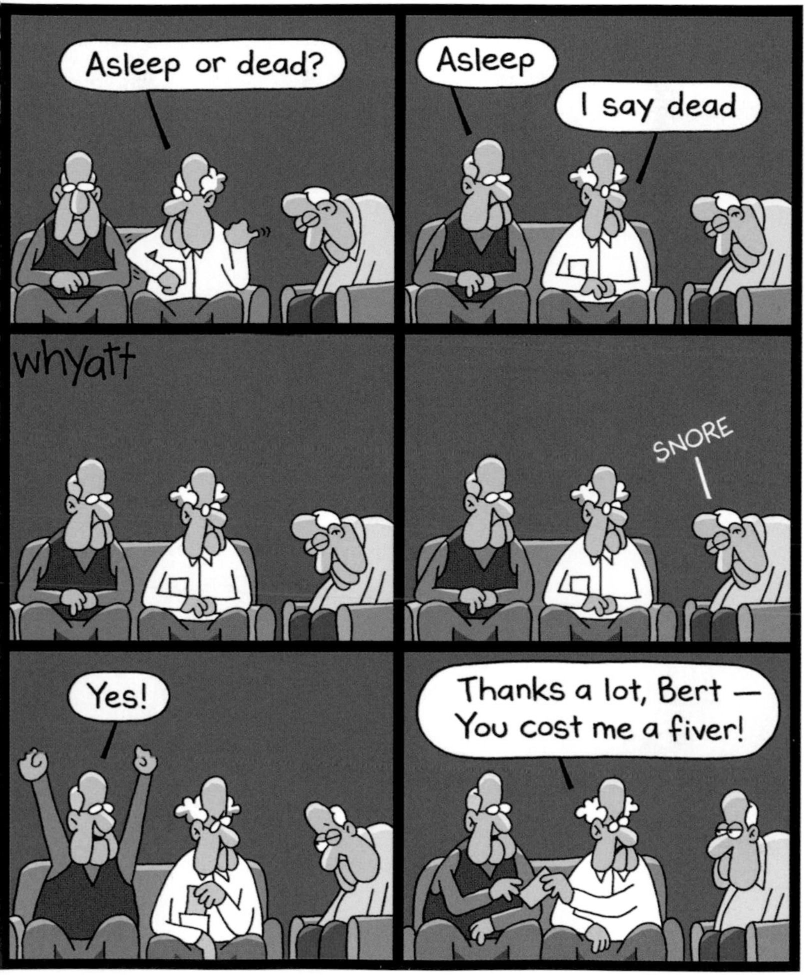
Asleep or dead?
Asleep
I say dead
whyatt
SNORE
Yes!
Thanks a lot, Bert —
You cost me a fiver!

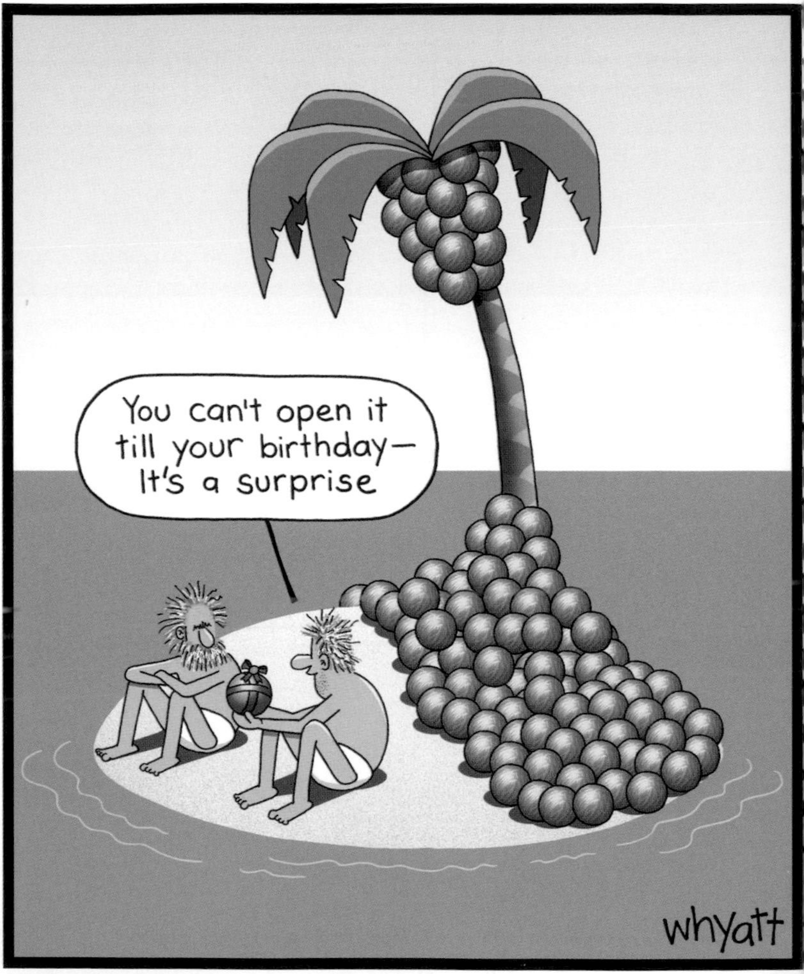
You can't open it till your birthday— It's a surprise
whyatt

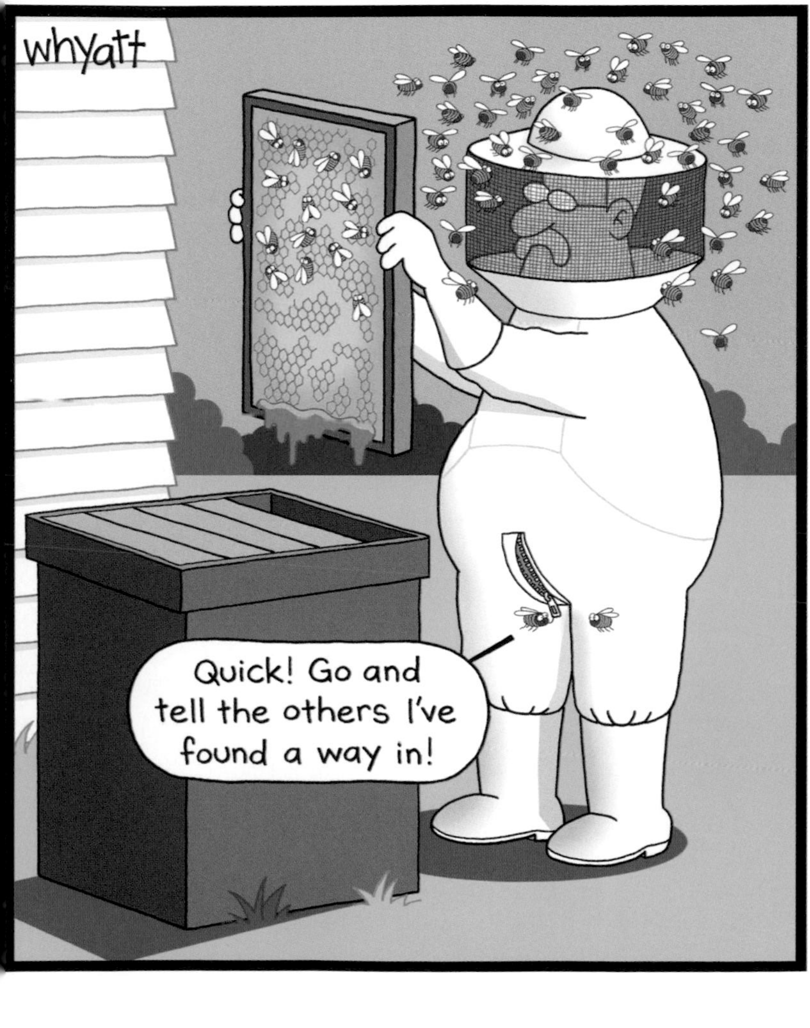
whyatt
Quick! Go and tell the others I've found a way in!

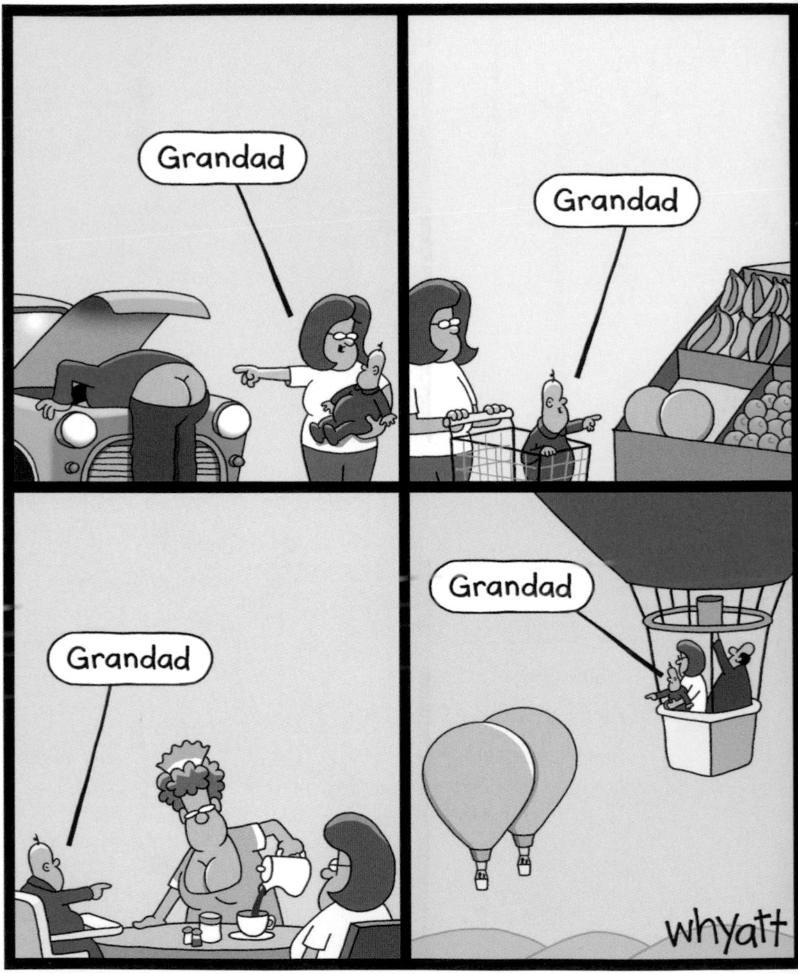
Grandad
Grandad
Grandad
Grandad
whyatt

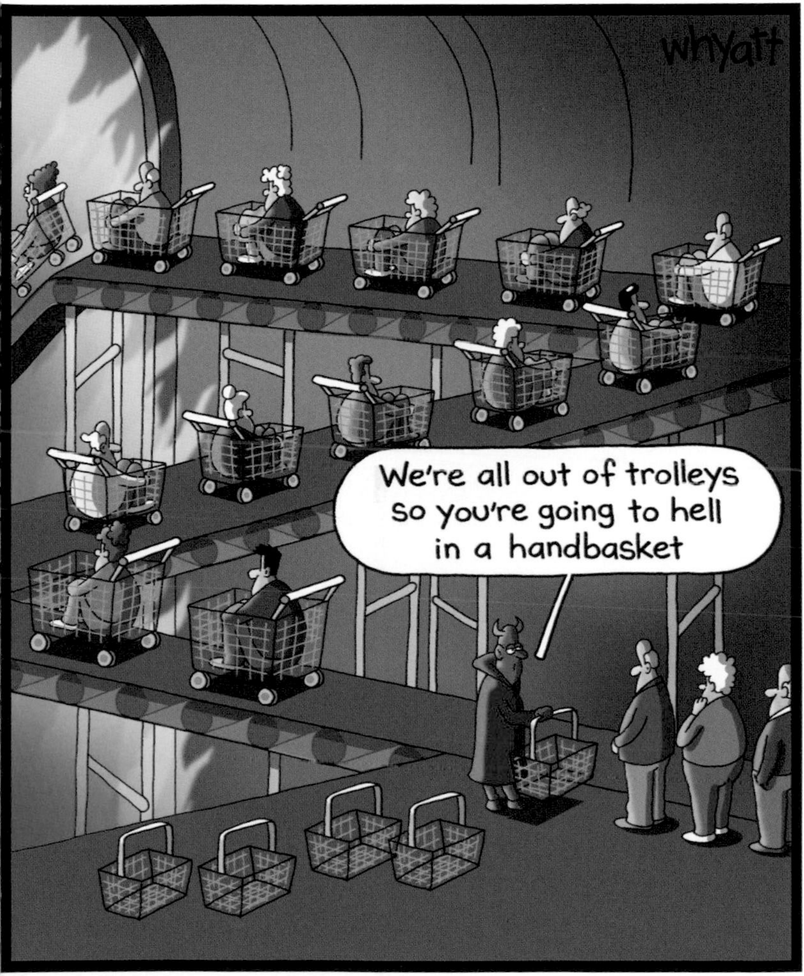
whyatt
We're all out of trolleys
so you're going to hell
in a handbasket

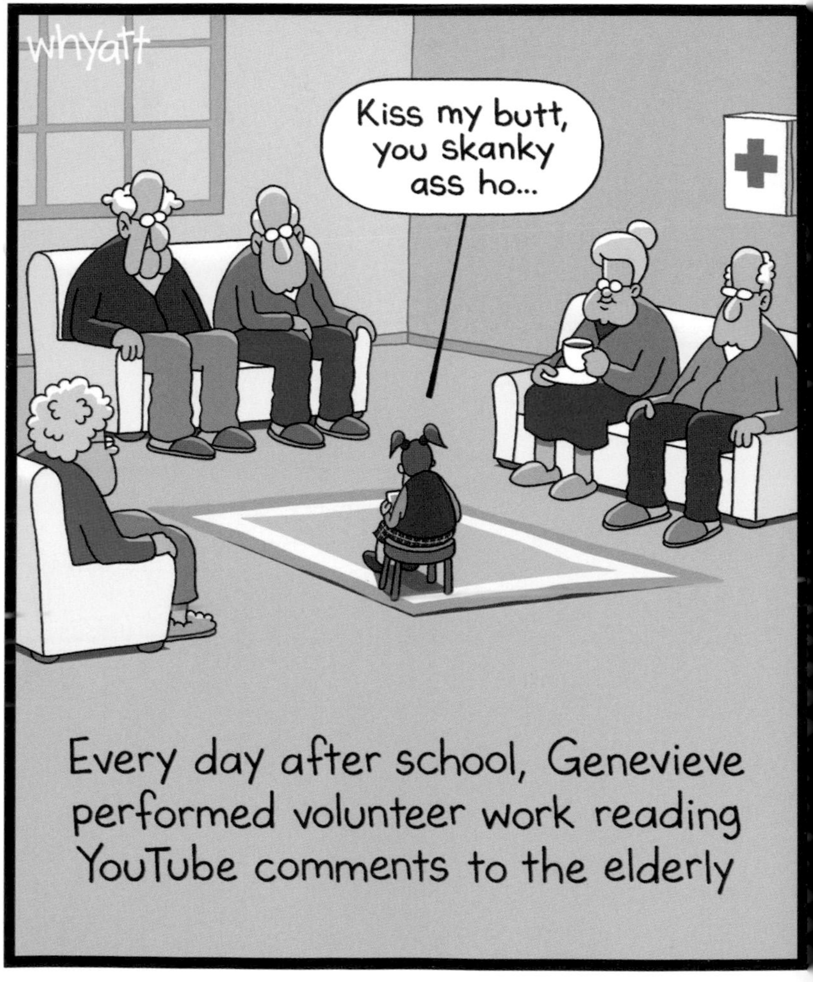
whyatt
Kiss my butt, you skanky ass ho...

Every day after school, Genevieve performed volunteer work reading YouTube comments to the elderly

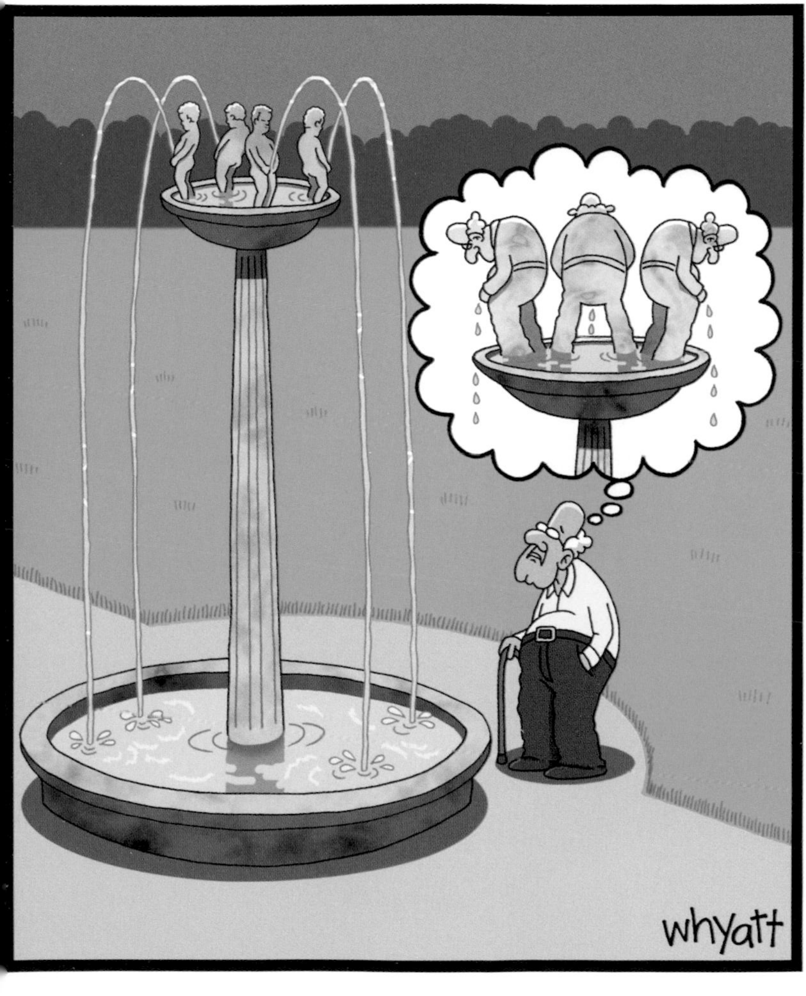
whyatt

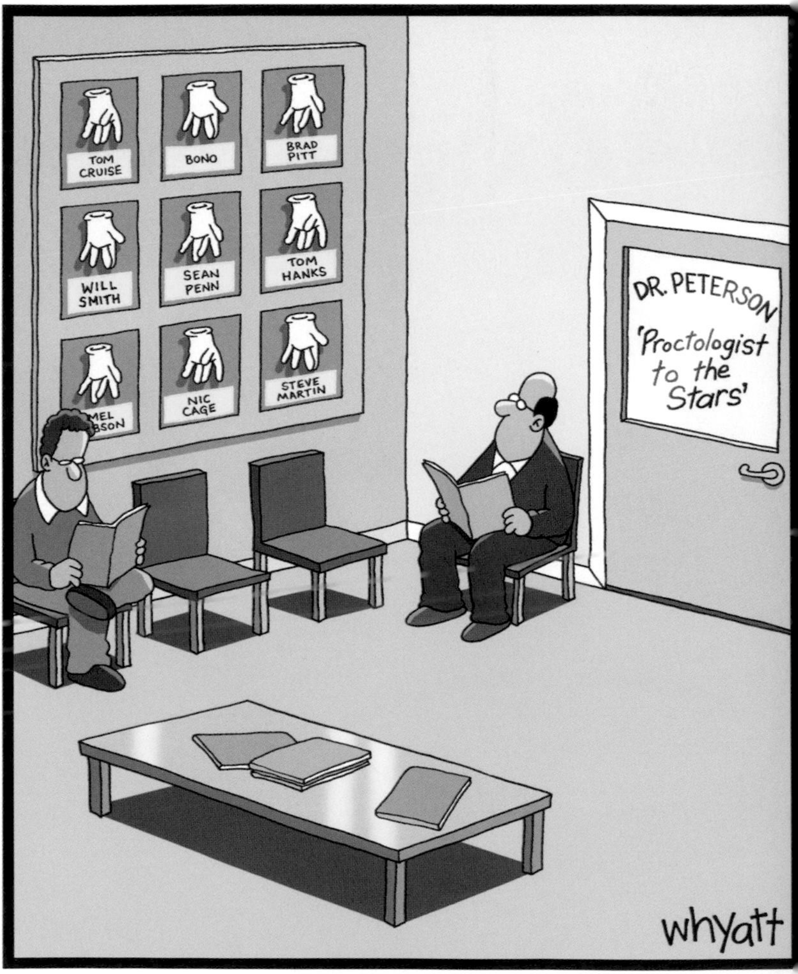
TOM CRUISE
BONO
BRAD PITT
WILL SMITH
SEAN PENN
TOM HANKS
NIC CAGE
STEVE MARTIN
DR. PETERSON
'Proctologist to the Stars'
whyatt

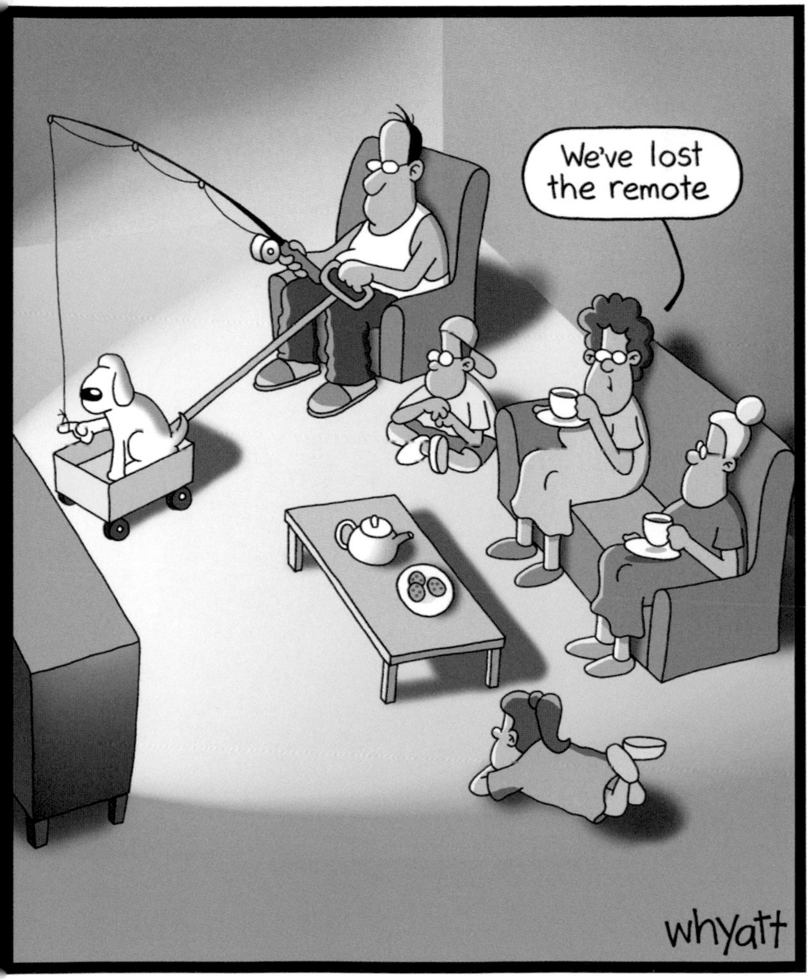
We've lost the remote
whyatt

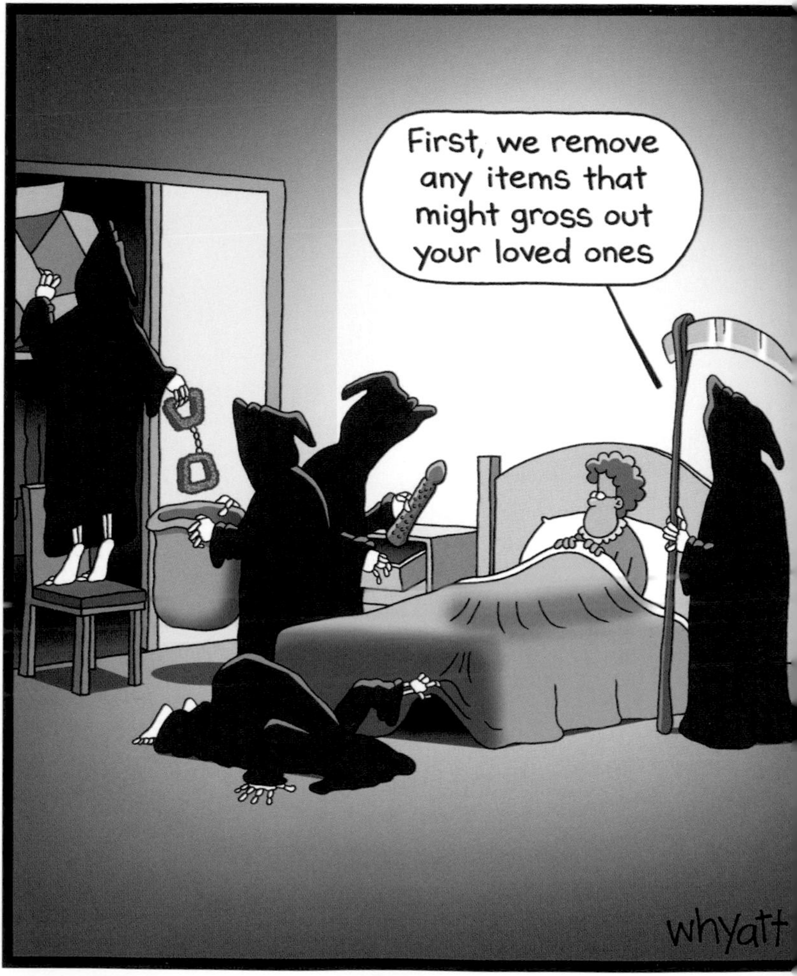
First, we remove any items that might gross out your loved ones
whyatt

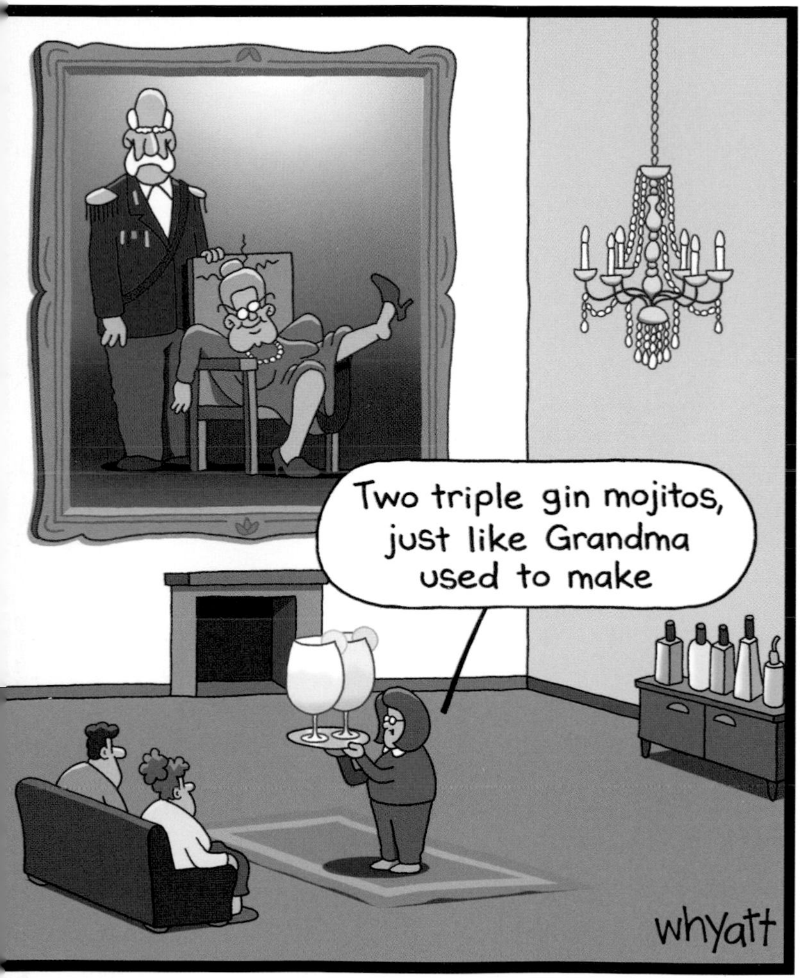
Two triple gin mojitos,
just like Grandma
used to make
whyatt

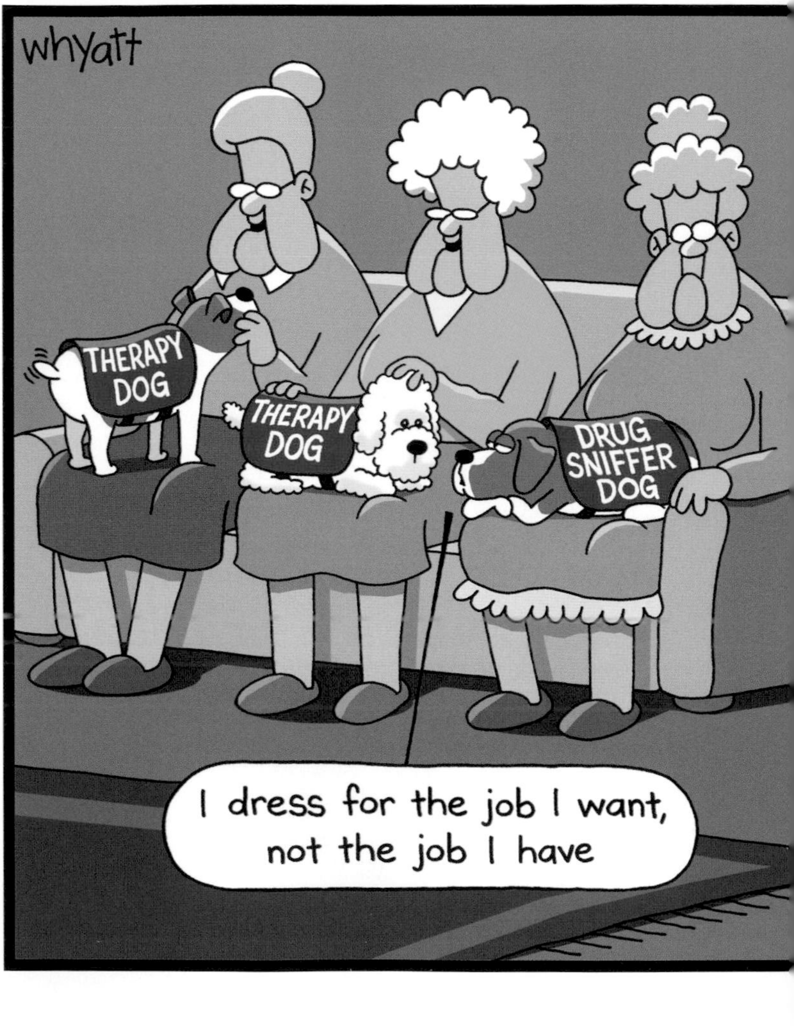
whyatt
THERAPY DOG
THERAPY DOG
DRUG SNIFFER DOG
I dress for the job I want, not the job I have

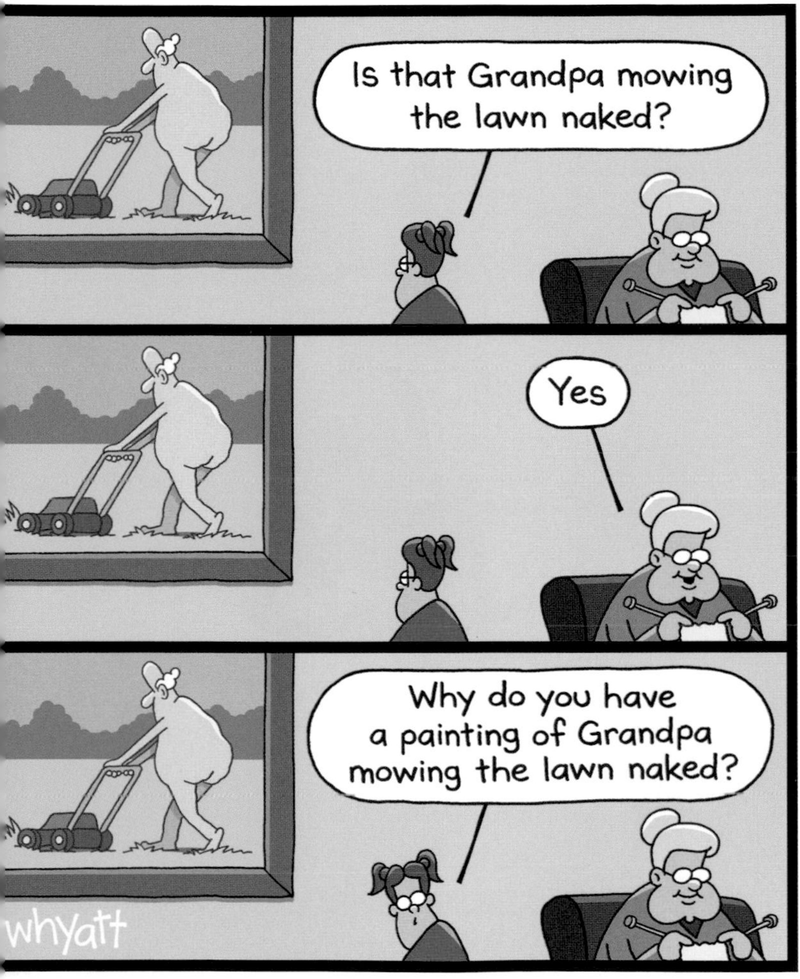
Is that Grandpa mowing the lawn naked?
Yes
Why do you have a painting of Grandpa mowing the lawn naked?
whyatt